rethinking

Forgiveness

Getting Ahead
Instead
Of Getting Even

Unless otherwise indicated all Scripture quotations are from The Holy Bible, New King James Version. Copyright © 1982 by Thomas Nelson, Inc. Used by permission.
All pre-chapter quotes were found on the internet.

Printed in U.S.A.

EarthenWare Publishing, Inc.
P.O. Box 95
Kennedale, Texas 76060

ISBN 978-0-9843421-0-5

www.forgiveandbless.com

Dedication

This book is dedicated to my wife—
the proof of Proverbs 18:22.

Thanks

No one does anything by himself. First of all, I would like to thank all those who have heard, received and put into practice this message of forgiveness. Your testimonies and support have helped to sustain me. Next, my undying gratitude is due to those who have prayed and stood with me to help see this project to completion. I am especially grateful to those who have helped with the practical details of turning the spoken word into the written. And then there are those who bought copies, sight unseen, and enabled this book to come to publication. "Blessed is he who does not see and yet believes."

To all of you: May the Lord reward your kindness and make a way for you and prosper·you.

Table of Contents

Part 1 Rethinking Forgiveness

Part 2 The Book of Blessings

Rethinking

Forgiveness

Life is an adventure in forgiveness.

Norman Cousins

Introduction

THE WELL-WORN MAXIM "don't get mad, get even" may play well in novels and movies, but revenge seldom works out in real life. It always costs too much and never satisfies the way you expect. Besides, revenge does not get you even. Returning evil for evil simply escalates the conflict and draws the parties deeper and deeper into the kingdom of darkness.

This book is based on the teachings of Christ. If you have any interest in what Jesus said concerning forgiveness, then the perspective given in this book may greatly change some of your thinking.

I discovered a very simple concept at a time when I needed it most. In the scripture, the Greek translation for the verb *to forgive* literally means *to remit*, or *to pay in full*. We dismiss a person's debt to us when we forgive him, and forgiving brings his account to zero. Revenge doesn't even the score; it only increases our indebtedness. The only real way to get even is to forgive. However, our emotions and our memories will not let us stay at zero, so we enter the cycle of forgiving, remembering, forgiving again, remembering again, and so on, over and over. This tormenting cycle eventually causes many of us to lose hope. To move past zero we must put something into the offender's account. The simple solution comes when we add a blessing after we forgive him. It really is that simple, and in this book you will discover the practical applications of forgiving and blessing. In these tandem acts we find the key to real freedom.

I hope that you will begin to implement what you learn here. I know that the practice of forgiving and blessing will change your life, just as it has changed mine and the lives of many others who have heeded this message.

**Forgiveness
is a funny thing.
It warms the heart
And cools the sting.**

William Arthur Ward

Getting Started

MY SISTER HAD HER TONSILS removed when I was five years old. In those days doctors would routinely remove a child's tonsils as a solution for chronic ear or upper respiratory infections. When I heard of this operation, I wanted to know all about it. Even at that early age my need to know went beyond normal curiosity, and after I had relentlessly questioned my mother, she finally found a way to explain it to me.

"We're going to take your sister to Dr. Tepper's office," she said.

This news excited me. Although most children hate pediatricians because of the poking and pinching and sticking of needles that goes on in their examination rooms, I loved Dr. Tepper, our pediatrician. Thanks to his waiting room, I have no bad memories of him. The people and places we know as little children sometimes grow small when we ourselves get bigger, but Dr. Tepper's waiting room still looms large in my memory. As big as an airplane hangar, with the walls lined with what seemed to be hundreds of lighted aquariums filled with the most extraordinary creatures, that room stunned and delighted my imagination. But the most wonderful thing of all was the model train in a vast layout of a familiar landscape under a glass dome. I recognized the town alongside the river as the same town I had seen from our car window as we would ride along Crest Road. I had been to Point Park on the mountain on the other side of the valley, and I knew the name of the other mountain, too. I recognized this scale model as my home town — my world in a size I could handle.

The little train waited, its engine and coal car ready to start its journey; waited for me to come and push the red button to send it on its way pulling the boxcars, hoppers and passengers cars followed by the little red caboose, out of the station, out of the town, across the river, around the mountain and through the forest before returning home again.

"We're going to take your sister to Dr. Tepper's office," my mother explained, "and in a room down in his basement they will put her on a table. Then the nurse will put a mask on her…"

"Wait, wait," I said. "What kind of a mask?"

"Well, uh, it's like a space mask, I suppose. And then…" And then, I never heard another word. Doctor Tepper would send my sister into space.

Despite my best efforts, I couldn't get a word out of her when she came home after the operation. I wanted to know what happened, but she stayed mum. Possibly my mother had instructed her not to say anything, but more likely my overwhelming and overbearing curiosity taxed her into silence.

I readied myself for a trip into space, and the day soon came for me to have my tonsils taken out. When we got to the doctor's office, I ignored the aquariums. I didn't even look at the train. Eager to embark on an adventure beyond my imagination, I could not give these earthbound matters my attention. I knew about the moon and the stars, and I wanted to see them up close.

Decades later, when I look back, I can still see a nurse placing something like a mask on my face. Everything went gray, and I woke up mad. I had been robbed. I had never traveled into space before, but I knew I still hadn't left Earth. My anger left me with no recollection of a sore throat. I rejected the Jello and even the ice cream. They could not console me. Betrayed by the one person I trusted implicitly, I refused to even speak as I thought the unthinkable: My mother had lied to me.

In later years, when I would teach about forgiveness, I would tell this story to illustrate how children become easily and unintentionally wounded. One day the Lord convicted me that I had not really forgiven my mother for this incident. I thought I had. I had made light of it and turned it into an amusing anecdote, but I had never made the conscious decision to forgive her. When I told her that I had held this against her all these years, she said, "You wouldn't leave me alone about it, and I was just trying to shut you up." As an adult, I knew she was not to blame, but at the age of five I couldn't work that out. As I talked with my mother, I realized how this unforgiveness had affected my attitude toward her, and I had the opportunity to ask her forgiveness for some of the things I had done.

As we deal with our forgiveness issues, we usually must begin with our family relationships. Whether by divorce, desertion, or workaholism, a disappearing parent can cause much harm. Other hurts and wounds range from the unintentional betrayals of imperfect parents to horrific forms of abuse. This does not apply just to Mom and Dad either. Siblings, aunts, uncles, cousins, and even friends of the family can hurt us too.

Children tend to blame themselves when wounded by the ones they love. They begin to think, "I must deserve to be treated this way." We form the perception of our value as human beings at an early age, and these judgments can stay with us into adulthood. If treated as worthless, children will begin to perceive themselves as worthless, and then act on this assumption by becoming people pleasers in the attempt to become acceptable, or by outright rebellion, believing that they can never measure up. By forgiving these offenses and the offenders who committed them we may begin to secure our freedom from the injuries of our past and to see God's redemption in our present.

However, starting with the family can sometimes overwhelm us. Once, after I had finished speaking about forgiveness, I stepped into a conversation between a friend of mine and his son, a young man in his mid-twenties. His mother had abandoned their family when he was eleven or twelve.

"Is the Lord speaking anything to you about your Mom?" the father asked.

"No," the young man said. "I'm thinking about my roommate who left and didn't pay his part of the rent."

It takes faith to forgive. When not ready to deal with the big issues, we must seek the Lord to find a starting place. We must ask Him first to convict us of any unforgiveness, and then begin to work from His list. Walking in forgiveness fulfills His desire and purpose for us.

That is why Jesus said "...love your enemies, bless those who curse you, do good to those who hate you, and pray for those who spitefully use and persecute you, that you may be sons of your Father in heaven..."[1] Our calling, our destiny is to be like Jesus, with the very character and nature of God,

Himself.

I found that I could not write the ultimate and all-inclusive book on forgiveness, but I do want to introduce you to an element of forgiveness that I think has been overlooked. I discovered it at a critical time when I felt that I had to forgive or die. As a Bible teacher for many years, I had often taught about forgiveness, but in the time of my greatest crisis, my teaching and my understanding failed me. The common teaching about forgiving left me stranded in my pain.

As I studied the definition of the Greek word translated to forgive, I saw something I had missed. This indispensable element altered almost everything I knew about forgiveness and it irrevocably changed my life and the lives of those with whom I've shared it.

I hope to show in the simplest terms possible how to forgive someone and keep him forgiven—in other words, how to forgive and make it stick. You will discover how to get off that merry-go-round of torment: the memory, the pain of the memory, and the coping that never really brings healing. Time does not heal our wounds. It only insulates us from them. Time can dim the pain, but those wounds, hidden like a cancer, can kill us. Only by applying the Blood of Jesus, and extending the grace of God to others, can we enjoy total freedom. Forgiveness does not rehash the past. It brings redemption in the present, opens the doorway to our future and lavishes upon us all the great blessings that the

Lord has in store for us now in this life and in the one to come.

We shall see that God has authorized us to forgive, and because He has, we can surely do it. We will also see what awaits us when we do not forgive. We will learn how to use that missing element to take us beyond forgiving into the victory won for us at Calvary.

Forgiveness is a universal issue. Just as we all have sinned against God and need His forgiveness, we all have been sinned against and need to forgive others. Since God is conforming each of us into the image of His Son, we must learn to walk in forgiveness. The capacity to forgive displays the very essence of God, and withholding it demonstrates everything foreign to Him. Nothing can be regarded as more fundamental than forgiveness. As bedrock Christianity, it is more important than doctrine, more important than creed, more important than church, and even more important than family, since forgiveness has the power to keep families together and unforgiveness has the power to break them apart. At the heart of our relationship with God and as an essential ingredient of healthy relationships with those around us, forgiveness can change lives and alter the course of history. The lack of it brings great devastation.

Forgiveness is an act of the will, and the will can function regardless of the temperature of the heart.

Corrie Ten Boom

Authorized
to Forgive

GOD IS GREATER than all things and all people, and a word or commandment from Him carries all of His authority and power. He said, "light be," and light was. He didn't explain it. He didn't describe it. He spoke it, and it came into being. With all of man's searching and all of the knowledge he has gained, he has yet to know all the properties and mysteries of the light that God created with a single word.

When we receive a command from the Lord, it is not a matter of should we, but rather will we? If He tells us to do it, we have the authority to do it. We may not at first understand how to respond in obedience, but the commandment itself delegates to us the necessary authority to carry it out. But authority does not stand alone. An associated responsibility always accompanies it. In fact, responsibility comes first — no responsibility, then no authority needed or given. This may seem obvious, but remarkably, people often want some authority without its corresponding responsibility. When Jesus tells us to forgive, we know He has given us two things — both the authority and the responsibility to forgive.

Did you know that you have a ministry and the authority to fulfill it? Actually you have more than one ministry. Each of us is given grace according to the gift of Christ,[1] and that grace enables us to fulfill what God has given us to do. While we all have a unique calling, we all also share a common and initial ministry.

Consider this passage:

2 Corinthians 5:17-19

17 Therefore, if anyone is in Christ, he is a new creation; old things have passed away; behold, all things have become new. 18 Now all things are of God, who has reconciled us to Himself through Jesus Christ, and has given us the ministry of reconciliation, 19 that is, that God was in Christ reconciling the world to Himself, not imputing their trespasses to them, and has committed to us the word of reconciliation.

This scripture tells us that we have been given the ministry of reconciliation. Simply put, in Christ,

God forgives. To "not impute their trespasses to them" means to forgive them. I would like for you to notice three things in these verses:

1. God in Christ

2. New Creations

3. Forgiveness

We will see these principles again in John 20:19-23. I encourage you to look up this passage in your Bible. I will not quote these verses directly, but I will tell you the story.

Several women saw Jesus early in the morning of the day He was resurrected. Peter saw Him later, and in the afternoon He met two of His disciples on the road to Emmaus. After that encounter, they immediately walked back to Jerusalem, and joined the others locked away in the upper room.

There Jesus appeared to them and said, "Peace be with you."

During His earthly ministry, Jesus often gathered His disciples around Him away from the crowds to speak to them of the Kingdom of God. That evening in the upper room He met with them in private as He once did. He showed them His hands and His side and spoke peace to them again. Then He said, "As the Father has sent me, I also send you." This statement corresponds to the first item on our list from 2 Corinthians 5. God is in Christ, and in the same way the Father sent Jesus, Jesus now sends His disciples.

With that He breathed on them and said, "Receive Holy Spirit."

Does the Bible speak anywhere else of God breathing on man? How about Genesis? God formed man out of the dust of the ground, and breathed the breath of life into his nostrils.[2] God breathed His Spirit into a well-sculpted but lifeless form, and man came alive. These men in the upper room did not need to be created, but when Jesus breathed on them, they became new creations.

The Hebrew word *ruach* appears in our English Bible translation in three different ways: breath, wind, and spirit. The New Testament Greek word *pneuma* is translated in exactly the same manner. Words such as pneumonia and pneumatic have this Greek word as their root.

Jesus breathed on His disciples in that upper room, and they received His breath and His spirit — His *pneuma*. When we receive the new birth, we receive the Spirit of Christ, and as the Scripture says, "If any man does not have the Spirit of Christ, he is not His."[3] Just as God breathed life into a lump of clay and man became a living soul, Jesus breathes His Spirit into us, and we become new creations. We, who were once dead in our trespasses and sins, now live in Him because He has breathed His Spirit into us.

When Jesus breathed on them these disciples became new creations, and although they had walked with Him for more than three years and had seen myriads of miracles, they had never experienced anything like this. For us, as well as for them, life in God begins with this impartation, and once He had made them new creations, what did Jesus say to them?

> John 20:23 If you forgive the sins of any, they are forgiven them; if you retain the sins of any, they are retained.

The very first directive Jesus gives His disciples concerns forgiveness. He put forgiveness at the top of the list of His post-resurrection instructions to His disciples. You have surely heard that old cliché about putting first things first. Jesus did just that. He told them the most significant thing first.

Whoever we forgive, they are forgiven. Very simple. He does not say that whoever we ask God to forgive will be forgiven. It is who *we* forgive, and that's a distinction that demands attention. We must forgive, and because Jesus tells us to do it, we *can* do it. Now, we may not be able to absolve someone of all their sins, but we can certainly forgive him for those offenses committed against us. No matter how difficult the task may seem, we have been given the capacity to forgive.

Whoever's sins we retain, they are retained. When we don't forgive someone we hold that person's sin. We do not hold him in his sin, but we hold his sin in us. I have enough problem with my own sin; I do not need to hold someone else's. When sin has fully run its course, it brings forth death.[4] By refusing to forgive, we embrace and bind to ourselves a cancer that will eventually take our lives.

Remember our list from 2 Corinthians: God in Christ, new creations, and forgiveness. That passage in 2 Corinthians perfectly describes what happened in the upper room with Jesus. He came, and said, "In the same way that the Father has sent me, I am sending you." Next he made them new creations, and then, He gave them their first ministry.

We may have a ministry of preaching, teaching, intercession, service, or one of the many other ministries the Bible speaks of, but any of those ministries is in addition to the first one we received. The first ministry of every Christian is walking in forgiveness.

The Son of Man

Luke 5 highlights a dramatic demonstration of the authority to forgive. A paralyzed man's friends bore him on a stretcher to a home meeting to see Jesus. Because of the crowd they were unable to get the man through the door, so they carried him to the roof, removed the tiles and lowered him down in front of the Master. When Jesus saw their faith, He said to the paralyzed one, "Man, your sins are forgiven."

When the scribes and the Pharisees heard this they said, "Who is this that says He can forgive sins? Only God can forgive sins." Have you heard that message? "Only God can forgive sins?"

Jesus knew their thoughts, and He said this, "Which is easier to say? 'Rise up and walk,' or 'your sins are forgiven?'" And then He said, "So that you may know that the Son of Man has authority on earth to forgive sins, I say to you, 'Take up your bed and walk'." The man stood up, picked up his belongings and left.[5]

Now, who is the Son of Man? When I ask that question, almost everyone answers "Jesus." Well, of course He is. But does the Bible call anyone else besides Jesus the "Son of Man?" Certainly. As God questioned Ezekiel about the valley of dry bones, He asked him, "Son of man, can these bones live?"[6]

The phrase "son of man" is probably capitalized in your Bible, but the original language does not make such a distinction. In New Testament Greek, that phrase literally means the child of a human being, and the beginning of verse 24 may be literally translated as: "So that you may know that the child of a human being has authority on earth to forgive sins…"

Are you one of those: a child of a human being? Of course, we all are. So Jesus healed that man and Luke recorded it in scripture so that we could know that we, the children of human beings, have authority on earth to forgive each other.

Resentment is like drinking poison and waiting for the other person to die.

Carrie Fisher

The Terrible Parable

T O OBTAIN A CLEAR understanding of the importance of forgiveness, we should first examine how God treats those who refuse to forgive. The most startling example is in the passage I call the Terrible Parable. If you have read any of the New Testament, then you surely know this passage.[1] I gave it this title because this passage clearly shows what we can expect to happen to us when we do not choose to forgive.

Jesus speaks about forgiveness in Matthew 18. In verse 21, Peter utters the question on everyone's mind. "How many times do I have to forgive," he asks, "seven times?" This seems like a reasonable amount of forgiveness, and seven is a very spiritual number. After all, how long do I have to put up with this sort of behavior? When is enough, *enough*? Jesus' answer in the next verse may have surprised Peter, but its implications are even more surprising. "Not just seven," Jesus says, "but up to seventy times seven."

Having to forgive four hundred ninety times requires a process, not merely one event. It means that I must continue to relate to the offender. If I quit forgiving after seven times, I could cut this miscreant from my life and be done with him. But "seventy times seven?" — a tall order!

So in verse 23 Jesus begins the story of a man who, while forgiven a great debt himself, will not forgive another a much smaller one. "Therefore the kingdom of heaven is like a certain king who wanted to settle accounts with his servants."

Jesus starts by saying that the "Kingdom of Heaven is like..." Please note that this story does not merely make a single point. Webster's on-line dictionary defines a parable as "... usually a short story that illustrates a moral attitude or a religious principle."[2] This long held and widely accepted definition does not accurately describe the parables of Jesus. His parables take us far beyond the emphasis of one or more principles. When He says, "The kingdom of heaven is like...," we can trust that what follows gives us an actual and accurate description of the Kingdom: what it looks like and how it operates. He speaks of "a certain King that wants to settle accounts with His servants." When Jesus says a *certain* King, He doesn't mean just any old king. He has someone specific in mind. This story shows us more than the importance of forgiving. This is the reality of the Kingdom: a true picture of how the Kingdom of God functions in respect to forgiveness.

As the king began to settle accounts, He found a man who owed ten thousand talents. Commentators usually speak of this amount in contemporary terms, often giving it a dollar value. Speculation about the size of the debt varies, depending on the commentary and the date of its publication. The value of money changes with time, and a dollar today will not buy what it would ten years ago. To grasp the enormity of this debt, it would help to translate it into terms that we can understand.

In the time of Jesus' earthly ministry, Rome ruled the western world, and He probably spoke in terms of the talents of that time, rather than Old Testament times. One denarius equaled one day's wage, and eighty-four denarii equaled one Roman pound, or libra. (We get the English abbreviation for pounds — lbs. — from this Latin word.) One hundred libras equalled one Roman talent. Figure the math. Ten thousand talents multiplied by one hundred pounds multiplied by eighty-four denarii equals eighty-four million days' wages. Look at the number: 84,000,000. Multiply what you make in a day times eighty-four million to see the real amount of this debt in contemporary terms. If a day's wage equaled one hundred dollars, then this man would have owed 8.4 billion dollars.

Since the servant understandably could not pay, the king decided to have him sold, along with his wife, children, and all of his personal possessions, resulting in negligible impact on this great debt. However it would make a big difference to the servant. He stood to lose everything, not only his possessions, but himself and his family too. So what did he do?

The servant fell down before the king and said, "Master, have patience with me, and I will pay you all." This desperate servant made a commitment he obviously could never keep. He simply would not live long enough to repay eighty-four million days' wages.

Moved with compassion, the Master released the servant and forgave him the entire debt. We can safely assume that this servant knew what he owed and had probably lived in fear of discovery, but the king's accounting freed him of the great effort to keep his financial failure concealed: no more covering, no more evasion, and best of all, no more debt. What a relief! If the story ended here, then it would have a happy ending.

However, this same servant went out and found one of his fellow servants who owed him one hundred denarii, one hundred days' wages. The first servant began to strangle the second, demanding, "pay me what you owe." The second servant fell down at his feet and begged him, saying, "Have patience with me, and I will pay you all."

Notice that the second servant did and said exactly the same thing as the first servant when confronted with his debt, but one small thing marks the difference between these two. In no way could Servant #1 ever repay what he owed, but given time, Servant #2 could repay this manageable debt of one hundred denarii. If he only paid one day's wage a week the debt could be repaid in less than two years.

Unforgiveness says, "You owe me," and really nothing else. So in the parable, the first servant had the second thrown into prison. I'm not sure I understand the thinking behind debtor's prisons. They had been around for centuries, and imprisonment for indebtedness remained a practice in England until abolished in 1869. Perhaps societies considered non-payment of debt as fraud, and therefore, a jailable offense. While in prison a person couldn't earn enough money to pay off the debt, so perhaps incarceration would pressure the debtor's family into bailing him out. Anyway, since the first servant couldn't immediately collect his money, he threw the second servant into jail.

This did not go unnoticed. When the other servants saw what had happened, they reported it to the Master. The Master called him and said to him, "You wicked servant! I forgave you all that debt because you begged me. Should you not also have had compassion on your fellow servant, just as I had pity on you?" And so the Master, in his anger toward the man, threw him into prison, had him tortured, and reinstated his debt.

The next verse, the last verse of this story, adds the terrible to the parable. Jesus says:

> 35 So My heavenly Father also will do to you if each of you, from his heart, does not forgive his brother his trespasses.

Take a close look at this principle where Jesus said that the Father would do the same to us if we would not forgive. Notice that Jesus speaks in terms of family: the Father and the brothers and does not address lost people. He does not warn what God would do to the unsaved if they don't forgive. He explains what the Father will do to His children if they don't forgive one another. If you have a problem with this, if it disturbs your theology, please take it up with Jesus. He said it, not me.

There are other scriptures that mirror this teaching. Luke 6:37-38 perfectly exemplifies what happened to this unforgiving servant.

> 37 Judge not, and you shall not be judged. Condemn not, and you shall not be condemned. Forgive, and you will be forgiven.
>
> 38 Give, and it will be given to you: good measure, pressed down, shaken together, and running over will be put into your bosom. For with the same measure that you use, it will be measured back to you.

Servant #1 put Servant #2 in prison, and soon he

found himself imprisoned, enduring torture, with his debt reinstated. What he gave he received in return, clearly with a good measure, pressed down and shaken together.

Some Observations

First, Jesus begins by giving a description of the Kingdom. His very words, "Therefore, the Kingdom of God is like…" reveal a reality, an actual description, and not just a story to scare us into forgiving one another. This actually happens.

Second, mercy awaits those who ask. The King, full of compassion, releases and forgives.

Third, unforgiveness causes grief and a righteous testimony rises against it. Remember the fellow servants saw what happened and went and testified to the master. If you walk in unforgiveness, you may not be able to see it, but others can, and a testimony rises to God about it. In His nature, God freely forgives, and I think that we should try to understand how much He hates unforgiveness.

Fourth, the master becomes angry at the one who will not forgive. Take note of this key point. I have searched the Bible, and I can find no other place where it states that God will be angry with His children — at least not since Jesus died on the cross. Do you think that God becomes angry at us because of our sin? He may deal with us firmly, but in love, not anger. Jesus died for our sins, paying for them all with His precious blood. Because of His Son's sacrifice, the Father loves to forgive sin. Sin does not provoke God's anger toward His children, but their unforgiveness does. Now these are some strong words.

Fifth, if we have unforgiveness, the Father not only becomes angry, He reinstates our debt. Remember that the master put the unforgiving servant in prison and said that he would not be released until he repaid everything he owed, just as if he had never received forgiveness in the first place.

Jesus explained only one part of what we call the Lord's Prayer. He didn't explain the Power, the Glory, or the Kingdom. He simply said, "If you do not forgive others, your Heavenly Father will not forgive you." With God as our Heavenly Father, we have already received His forgiveness. But Jesus plainly said in Matthew 6:15 that the Father won't forgive us if we don't forgive. God re-instates our debt when we choose not to forgive.

Sixth, since the unforgiving servant cannot be freed until he pays everything he owes, how will he ever get out of prison? How can he pay such a debt? Obviously he can't. However, the Master did not imprison Servant #1 because of his debt, but because he put Servant #2 in prison. To be free of prison and torment we must release and forgive all those who we still hold in debt to us. To get out of jail, we must let the other person out first.

Seventh, what about those tormentors? Are they the good guys or the bad guys? Are they friends or enemies? Did you see that the Master delivered the servant to these tormentors? The scripture doesn't say that God let down a protective hedge so that the prisoner became vulnerable to the attack of the enemy. It says that He delivered him into the hands of the enemy specifically for torture. These are very strong words, indeed, and surely some of the most sobering in scripture.

Fortunately, I have never endured physical torture, and I hope that you haven't either. Women tell me that childbirth brings the greatest pain, but those who have passed a kidney stone say *that* pain eclipses all others. It is physiologically impossible for me to experience the first, and by God's mercy I hope never to experience the second. But I have had a toothache.

A toothache hurts, and stopping the pain becomes our one goal in life. When we have a toothache, do we think about how good our life is, or about how much God loves us? Do we think about what a wonderful time we had last weekend, or what a wonderful time we'll have in the future? Do we think about our great job, or our wonderful children? Do we think about any of that? We think about that pain, and how we can ease it.

Many, many Christians live lives full of torment and torture for one reason, and one reason only: unforgiveness. These people fill our church communities. Talk to some people for two minutes and they get right to the subject of their pain along with who caused it. Sometimes those things happened five, ten, or twenty years ago. Time does not heal our wounds. It only insulates us from them. Until we forgive those who have wounded us, those hurts remain unhealed, even though we may not currently feel the pain.

Now you understand why I call this the Terrible Parable. With truly horrible consequences, unforgiveness stunts our growth and robs us of God's good intention for us, and eventually leaves us as imprisoned, tormented paupers.

But there is a way out, and it is not as hard as you might imagine.

**The one who pursues revenge
should dig two graves.**

Ancient Chinese Proverb

Symptoms of Unforgiveness

BEFORE WE LOOK at how we can get some relief from torment, we should examine some of the symptoms of unforgiveness. First, look at the three R's: recrimination, retribution, and revenge.

Recrimination means to answer an accusation with an accusation. If someone says something hurtful to us or about us, we often react and say something equally as hurtful in return. The frequent use of this defense mechanism may indicate that we have some unforgiveness.

Retribution (recompense) means the just, or deserved, punishment for an evil done. Sometimes we express the desire for retribution in this way: "I'll forgive you, because I know God will get you for what you've done to me." We want this person to pay, but we can never fully satisfy our desire for retribution. They could pay and pay, but it would never be enough.

Revenge means personally inflicting damage, injury, or pain, in return for the same received.

When we recriminate, we set ourselves up as the judge. Desiring retribution, we pronounce a sentence on our offender, and then we become their executioner, taking revenge for what they have done.

Do you see the progression here? Participating in this process has some unwelcome consequences. God has said, "Vengeance is mine; I will repay."[1] Doing any of these things places us on the Judge's bench, and He does not take kindly to anyone who would attempt to usurp His authority or take over His job.

After the three R's, the symptoms of unforgiveness take on two forms: external and internal symptoms. We observe external symptoms in our relationships and circumstances. We see internal symptoms in our thought processes and emotions.

External Symptoms

Avoiding certain subjects and the inability to talk about certain things without pain point to an unhealed wound, especially when we can't allow others to mention them in our presence.

Avoiding certain people or the impossibility of having more than a superficial conversation with them indicates that unresolved issues have hindered our relationship with them.

Unforgiveness that runs in your family and the constant squabbling among your relatives indicate that you may have grown up in an unforgiving environment. Tendencies run in families, and observing how our parents and their siblings interact can give us a clue about ourselves.

Strife and contention rate high among the symptoms of unforgiveness. Some people seem impossible to get along with, and sometimes we can find a good reason for the contention and discord in our relationship with them. But usually our intolerance reflects our attitude towards them. Even the simplest rivalry can indicate unrighteous judgment or unforgiveness.

Chronic financial problems point to deep-seated and abiding issues of unforgiveness. Everyone may experience straitened financial circumstances from time to time, but the constant year in year out, demeaning inability to get ahead finds its root in only one thing. Remember the Terrible Parable? If we harbor unforgiveness God does not stop blessing us. He has promised and His faithfulness endures. The blessing comes, but we never see it. Because we don't see it, we think He has stopped blessing us. The reinstatement of our un-repayable debt gobbles up the blessings of God and leaves us with prison wages: something to wear, a place to sleep, and a little something to eat. Many Christians never see God's full intention for them because they hold unforgiveness. If you want to get even, you will never get ahead.

Internal Symptoms

Inability to recognize other people's value and contribution shows up in disdain, contempt, spite, scorn or belittling. This symptom also includes viewing another's difficulty with delight.

Envy and jealousy bring confusion and every evil work.[2] Sometimes when we see others enjoying God's favor, we become envious and cannot rejoice with that person. Have you ever said, "Why him? Why not me? I'm just as spiritual as he is, probably more so." An unrighteous judgment, that sentiment reveals symptoms of unforgiveness and ingratitude.

Justifying ourselves should instantly sound an alarm bell. Any time we justify in our minds our unkind words or actions toward someone, we almost certainly have unforgiveness toward him or someone else who has treated us in a similar manner. When we meet someone and develop an instant dislike for him, he may remind us of someone else who has harmed us in some way. It may have nothing to do with the person we just met.

Anger tops the list of symptoms of unforgiveness. There are many causes for anger, but a constantly angry person has deeply embedded unforgiveness issues. Irrational anger reveals an especially obvious clue. I remember a Norman Rockwell illustration on the cover of an issue of *The Saturday Evening Post*. The first frame showed a man being chewed out by his boss. In the next frame, he goes home and chews out his wife. She then chews out their son, who in turn chews out the dog. Often the object of our anger differs from the source of it. When this happens we must ask the Lord to show us why we act this way.

Chronic or irrational fear strongly indicates unforgiveness, simply because fear has torment. Torment comes from tormentors, and the Father delivers us to them when we will not forgive. Mental health practitioners have documented and referenced well over 500 phobias, from ablutophobia, the fear of washing or bathing, to zoophobia, the fear of animals. The fear of anything qualifies as a phobia,[3] so the list could stretch into infinity. There is even a fear of phobias, phobophobia. But God has not given us a spirit of fear, and the only thing that authorizes fear to control our lives is our own unforgiveness.

Other symptoms may include ingratitude, independence, isolation and loneliness. If you feel trapped or imprisoned, tortured or tormented, or can't seem to forgive yourself, then consider unforgiveness as the source.

Not all of the above symptoms indicate unforgiveness, but displaying any of these should provoke us to pray. All of these symptoms indicate emotional hurts and may lead us to finding unforgiveness. We can mask unforgiveness in so many ways and should never underestimate our capacity for self-deception.

Now for some good news.

**To forgive is to set
a prisoner free
and discover that the
prisoner was you.**

Philip Yancey

The Zero
Principle

S O FAR WE HAVE SEEN that God has
authorized us to forgive, and we have also
discovered what happens when we don't.
But how do we do it, exactly? How do we forgive
and make it stick?

A computer program usually has something
called a loop. As part of a set of instructions used
to accomplish a repetitive task, a program can go
to the loop, run it as many times as it needs, and
then exit the loop, after producing the desired
results. But sometimes the program can get stuck
in that loop and never finish its task. Our efforts to
forgive sometimes seem like that. An offense comes

and hurts and wounds us. We experience all the emotion and reasoning that comes with the pain. We struggle to forgive and may even gain a measure of peace, but then we see that person; or someone mentions their name; or we just simply remember the event; and we return to the beginning of the cycle and go through it all over again.

In our efforts to get off this merry-go-round, we eventually find ways to cope. We avoid that person. We shut them from our minds. We try to blot out the memory of what happened. Or we make light of it by saying that we have forgiven them, and then we dismiss that person and that part of our lives. Then something triggers our memory, and we return to that cycle. Without always realizing it, we become exhausted and worn down and never actually get free. With the passage of time we may no longer feel the pain, and the memory of the offense begins to fade. But, as I said earlier, time does not heal our wounds; it only insulates us from them. After a while, the issue may subside from our daily, conscious lives and become buried deep in our memory, but it will remain there, lingering, and will not go away until fully addressed.

We never escape that endless loop, because forgiving is only half of the answer. The Greek word used in John 20:23 and translated as the verb to forgive, literally means to remit, or to pay in full. An account paid in full has a balance of zero.

Forgiving only gets us to zero. Even if we get there, we can't stay long, because our struggle depletes us and brings us little success. When we have the choice of remembering the offense or remembering nothing, which will we think about? As hard as we may try, we can't remember nothing. (I know it sounds like bad English, but not really.) Just try it. For the next thirty seconds, don't think about anything.

Many struggle with forgiveness because, unknowingly, they have made zero their goal. But who wants that kind of goal? If you worked all week, collected your check, paid your bills, and had nothing left over, would you jump for joy because you had nothing to show for your efforts?

Since God effectively and powerfully forgives, how does He do it? God and zero have absolutely nothing in common. Consider this verse:

Romans 8:32

He who did not spare His own Son, but delivered Him up for us all, how shall He not with Him also freely give us all things?

When Jesus died on the cross, He paid for our sins and brought our account to zero. But it did not end there. When God raised Jesus from the dead, He put a great blessing into our account. He freely gave us all things. Such a great blessing deposited enough into our account that nothing can reduce our account to zero, and it keeps us permanently out of the red.

To truly forgive, we must go beyond zero. We must begin to bless, just as God did when He forgave us. Genuine forgiveness has two parts:

forgiving brings us to zero, and blessing— the other half of forgiveness— creates a positive balance and blasts us out of the cycle of memory and pain.

"This person has severely harmed me," you might be thinking, "and I'm supposed to give them a blessing?" Consider another question first. Who benefits the most from forgiveness: the one who forgives, or the one forgiven? Who benefited the most when God forgave us: us or Him?

If you said "Him" you would be correct. While the forgiveness of our sins greatly benefited each of us, God obtained the greater benefit. He could only regain us by providing a way to forgive us, and He did not gain just one or two, but all who would accept His redemption. With the blood of Jesus remitting our sins, He bought us all for Himself.

Isaiah 43:25

> I, even I, am He who blots out your transgressions for My own sake; and I will not remember your sins.

We benefit the most when we forgive and bless those who have offended us. If we don't forgive, we hold onto their offense, and the anger and resentment that comes with it will bear the fruit of bitterness that will consume us, along with all that God has promised us. Until we forgive those who have offended us, we remain their victim. When we forgive and bless, we become a victor, and only a victor has the authority and power to forgive.

Our emotions often hinder us. If we wait until we feel like forgiving, we never will. Our emotions—

lagging indicators of our well-being— belong to the soul. If I follow my emotions, then I follow my soul and not my spirit. The sons of God are led by the spirit,[1] not by the soul. When we begin to bless, our emotions begin to change because we cannot long feel ill toward someone that we routinely bless.

At the end of the Terrible Parable, Jesus indicated that we must forgive from the heart.[2] We usually take this to mean that it has to be heart-felt. But I don't think He meant that. Paul tells us in Romans 10 that the heart is the organ of faith.[3] Forgiveness is an act of faith that requires a choice, not an emotion. By faith we must choose to forgive, regardless of how we feel about it. Regularly forgiving and blessing — in faith choosing to believe and act as God has directed us — will enable our souls to fall in line with our spirits and our disposition will greatly improve.

Forgive and Forget

The idea that "if we haven't forgotten, we haven't forgiven" shackles us to hopelessness. The doctrine of forgive and forget has become one of the greatest frauds ever perpetrated on the human race. This simple ploy of our enemy encourages us to attempt the impossible, and only brings us discouragement and defeat. Perhaps you have had this internal conversation with the Devil.

"Do you remember what they did to you?" he asks.

"Uh, yes I do," you reply.

"See there," he says. "You haven't forgiven them because you haven't forgotten."

You should not even attempt to forget a harm done. If someone offended you, it happened. Even if an imaginary offense causes a wound, to forget the offense is to deny the wound, and denial will not bring healing. Besides, not even God forgets. The scripture does not say that God forgets our sins. It says that He remembers them no more.[4] Just because God has forgiven us our past doesn't mean that He doesn't know who we were. He knows our history. He knows what we did. He doesn't deny it or pretend it didn't happen. He simply forgave us, and forgiveness brings a different perspective to everything. If all of our sins are totally forgotten, we would have no testimony, and our testimony is one of the three most powerful weapons we have against the enemy.[5]

God doesn't remember our sins because something else is on His mind. When God thinks of us, he does not think in terms of what it cost Him to forgive us. He thinks of us in terms of how He has blessed us. The blessing displaces the debt. Forgiving and blessing enables us to remember our past without the pain.

So when the Devil says, "Do you remember what they did to you?"

You can say, "Of course I remember. How could I forget? But I also remember that I have blessed them."

And if you really want to torque Ol' Slewfoot, you can say, "Thanks for reminding me to continue to bless this person." If you continue to bless the offender, I guarantee you that the Devil will soon quit reminding you of this matter.

No Vocabulary

Our greatest impediment to blessing consists of our lack of vocabulary and training. Ignorance has prevented us from acquiring this simple skill. I like to teach forgiveness to small groups because of the opportunity for practical application. By the time I start talking about the Zero Principle, the conviction of the Holy Spirit has become very strong, and almost everyone has begun to think about someone they need to forgive. When I ask, I always get a volunteer to walk through the process in front of the group.

First I ask who they need to forgive and why. Next I lead them through a simple prayer:

"Father, thank You for forgiving me of all my sins and for washing me clean with the blood of Jesus. I now, of my own free will, choose to forgive 'so-and-so' for 'this-and-that'."

Sometimes the "so-and-so" is a family member, and sometimes not. Sometimes the "this-and-that" is huge, and sometimes small. Usually my volunteer will get through this without much trouble. Even though deep hurts may bring a serious display of emotion, they usually understand the need for this part of the process. But when I explain that we must now go beyond forgiving, and put something into that person's account by giving them a blessing, they usually respond with a blank stare. They just don't know where to start.

Once, in a small group, I walked a woman through forgiving her ex-husband. They had two sons together, but he had left her for a younger woman. I led her through the prayer of forgiving, and then asked her to bless him. She had no clue how to begin.

"Obviously this man has problems in relationships," I said.

"Certainly," she agreed.

"So let's bless him with good relationships," I began, and she repeated this blessing after me. "May the Lord watch over him and bring to him the relationships that he needs. May they all be fruitful and satisfying, and may he have only those relationships that God intends for him to have."

She nodded in agreement.

"How about another blessing?" I asked. I could see that we were making progress, but she couldn't yet come up with a blessing on her own,

To pay alimony, child support, and maintain two families is expensive. "Can we bless him in his finances?" I asked.

"Oh, no," she said, "he's got enough money." Her response brought a chuckle from the group. I suspected that she was secretly pleased that he was bearing such financial burdens.

"We cannot move beyond the point where we stop blessing," I told her.

"All right," she reluctantly agreed, "but you'll have to help me."

So we blessed him — that he would be a generous man and choose the things that have high value. That he would be a man of integrity, to whom God could entrust the means to help others. That he would be known as a wise man, full of compassion.

As I looked at her face I could see her countenance lighten, and I knew something had changed in her.

"I have led you through two blessings," I said, "and I can see that you are feeling better. But now you have to come up with a blessing on your own."

As I watched, the compassion of a mother's heart welled up into her eyes, and she said, "I want him to be a good father."

She began to bless him with all the qualities of a good father, and as she finished, she smiled and laughed, her heart full of joy. We all could see that the anger and bitterness that had made her miserable had evaporated.

Balancing the Books

As we bless, we impart and deposit something into our beneficiary's account. Please view this verse in accounting terms:

2 Corinthians 5:20

Now then, we are ambassadors for Christ, as though God were pleading through us: we implore you on Christ's behalf, be reconciled to God.

We often think of this verse in terms of evangelism. We, as ambassadors, should beseech the lost to be reconciled to God. But Paul wrote this to believers, and this passage does not address the unbeliever. To reconcile, a bookkeeping term, means to balance the books. If we have a great blessing from God on one side of our ledger, and yet hold someone else's debt on the other, then we have an unbalanced account, and we are not reconciled to God.

Forgiveness, more a process than a mere event, begins with a decision. We must choose to forgive, and we must choose to bless. Most of us know about forgiving, but few have been trained to bless. Once we become practiced in this easily acquired skill, blessing becomes easy. This process will make us like the One who has forgiven us, the One who does not return cursing for cursing, and the One who returns good when evil is done.

**Without forgiveness,
there's no future.**

Desmond Tutu

Blessing

AFTER ALEXANDER THE GREAT conquered most of the then known world, Greek became the common language of the subjugated lands, and sometime between 300 and 200 BC, a group of seventy or so scholars translated the Hebrew writings we call the Old Testament into Greek. Many Jews had begun to lose their Hebrew language as they spread across the Greek Empire, and this translation enabled them to stay in touch with their sacred writings. It also allowed Gentiles to look into the Scriptures.

The concept of blessing, while central to Judaism, hardly existed in the Greek society. No equivalent Greek words could convey the full meaning of the Hebrew group of words for blessing, so the translators had to settle for something less than perfect.

Translated as the verb to bless, the Greek word, *eulogeo*, means to speak well of. The noun, *eulogia*, means fine speaking. We derive our English word eulogy from this, and it has come to mean the fine things we say about someone at their funeral. Sadly, we often take such memorial services as our only opportunities to say such things. This maintains the Greek concept, but totally fails the Hebrew understanding of blessing. The Scriptures maintain this greater idea throughout both the Old and New Testaments contexts.

The Scripture uses blessing as an act of transfer, either by word or action.[1] So when Jesus says, "Bless those that curse you, and do good to those that hate you," He means to speak well of those who speak ill of you, and do good to those who would bring you harm. The two injunctions demonstrate the very definition of "love your enemies."

The simple fact that Jesus told us to bless those who curse us conveys to us all the authority we need to add a blessing to those we forgive. But we don't have to wait for someone to offend us before we can give them a blessing — and why should we?

We can bless the people of God. Paul, the apostle, begins and ends each of his letters with a blessing, and the Scripture is filled with blessings from Genesis to Revelation. God told Abraham, "I will bless those that bless you and curse those that curse you, and in you all the nations of the earth will be blessed."

We can sometimes find ourselves in a very curious position. As the descendants of Abraham, whether naturally or by faith, we receive the blessing of God, and yet, at the same time, we may receive the cursing of God because we curse other descendants of Abraham. May it never be!

We can also bless our families. As Isaac lay dying, he called his oldest and favorite son to his bedside. He told Esau to bring him a stew made from fresh game, and after dinner he would bless him. Rebecca overheard the conversation between her husband and her eldest, and once Esau left on his hunt, she found her favorite son, and together they conspired to steal Esau's blessing. Jacob put on his brother's clothes, and with a dish his mother had made, went in to his near-sighted father.

Isaac blessed Jacob, thinking that he was Esau. When the true Esau reappeared, Rebekah and Jacob's deception angered and dismayed both him and his father. But Isaac understood something about blessing that few of us have grasped. The blessing stands. It cannot be revoked. Even though Isaac may have wanted to take back the blessing from Jacob and give it to Esau, he knew he couldn't. "I have blessed him," Isaac said, "and indeed he shall be blessed."[2] Here's what David said regarding God's blessing for him.

1 Chronicles 17:27

Now You have been pleased to bless the house of Your servant, that it may continue before You forever; for You have blessed it, O Lord, and it shall be blessed forever.

A curse can be broken. Jesus became accursed for us to free us from all curses. A blessing cannot be broken. Blessings endure. Once uttered, they stand, impossible to retrieve. God does not speak capriciously, saying one thing today and taking it back tomorrow. His promise is sure and His word immutable; He is not a man that He should lie.[3] God stands by His word, and He expects us to stand by ours.

The Lord has authorized us to bless. In fact, He has made us His partners and His agents of blessing in the earth. Through us He speaks and acts to impart blessing to a world in desperate need of it. We are His mouth and hands. When He says that the words that go forth from His mouth will not return until they accomplish what He sent them to do,[4] we can believe that our words of blessing, spoken on His behalf, behave in the same manner. Since He has empowered and authorized us to bless, He backs up our blessings as though He uttered them Himself.

In Numbers, Chapter 6, God tells Moses how to instruct Aaron in blessing the Israelites, resulting in this famous blessing:

The Lord bless you and keep you;

The Lord make His face shine upon you and be gracious to you.

The Lord lift up His countenance upon you and give you peace.

The Lord concludes His directive by saying, "So shall he (Aaron) put My name on the children of Israel."[5] Why wouldn't God just put His name on them Himself? As High priest, Aaron had the delegated authority to bless. There are things that only God can do, and there are things that He has given us to do. It is futile for us to attempt to do the things that only God can do, but it is foolish to think that He will step in and do the things that he has commissioned us to do. If we don't do them, they usually remain undone.

Our heavenly Father, the perfect parent, knows that we learn best by doing. When my sons were small and we had tasks to do, I often did not have the patience I should have had and did not allow them the time and room to do things imperfectly. I would step in, get the job done, and then go on to the next thing. Our Father does not do that. He lets us do it until we learn to do it well, never taking over the things He has given us to do.

Over the years I have learned how to bless. I have also had the privilege of helping others learn how to bless. Since example teaches best, I walk them through a couple of blessings, and then let them bless on their own. They usually become enthusiastic once they realize that the act of blessing, although a little awkward at first, really comes easily and has an immediate effect on them personally. I might help a little with vocabulary, but they catch on quickly and soon look for someone, anyone, to bless. The woman I spoke of earlier, who needed to forgive her ex-husband, models an example of this.

My wife and I have become convinced that blessing our children has had a far greater impact on them than just praying for them. If Aaron could put the name of the Lord on the children of Israel by blessing them, then we can put the name of the Lord on our children in the same way. "But Aaron was the High Priest," you might say. Yes, but God has made us a kingdom of priests.[6] God has given me the authority and responsibility to bless my children, and since He will not do what He has commissioned me to do, I have confidence that my blessings carry weight and that my words are spiritually effective. My blessings go and do what they were sent to do, and I believe they do not fall to the ground empty.

I know of no better example of the power and endurance of blessing than the story of Stephen. Stephen and Phillip, two of the first seven deacons, became evangelists, and they both had powerful, miraculous ministries. We have quite a record of Phillip's evangelistic exploits. The whole city of Samaria was saved when he came to town, but no account exists of anyone that Stephen led to the Lord. I don't doubt that he did, but the Scripture simply doesn't mention it.

Some of the religious leaders of the day began

to dispute with Stephen, and because they could not counter his wisdom with their arguments, they accused him of blasphemy and dragged him before the council. As Stephen spoke to the council members, they became furious and visibly agitated. Then Stephen had a vision. "Look!" he said. "I see the heavens opened, and the Son of Man standing at the right hand of God." To them this wild proclamation proved his blasphemy, and they became enraged. The story of Stephen begins in Acts 6:8 and continues to the end of Acts 7. Please read it there. I would like to recount here the series of events beginning in Acts 7:54 and discuss each of them individually.

Stephen sees Jesus standing at the right hand of God. This seems curious. When God raised Jesus from the dead, Paul tells us in Ephesians, He seated Him at His right hand. So what makes Jesus stand now in this story of Stephen?

In the Americas almost everyone knows baseball. Just imagine watching your home team. In the bottom of the ninth inning, with the bases loaded, you're down 3 to nothing. The count is 3 and 2, and your biggest hitter waits at the plate for surely the last pitch of the game. Who remains in his seat? Everyone stands to his feet, waiting for the next play. Jesus stood up to watch Stephen knock the ball out of the park.

Next, the religious leaders drag Stephen outside the city and begin to stone him. A zealous young man in the crowd looked on approvingly. He did not throw any stones, but he held the coats of those who did. He later created havoc among the church, dragging men and women from their homes and throwing them into prison.

As the mob stoned him, Stephen called on God, and said, "Lord Jesus, receive my spirit."

Then Stephen knelt down. Imagine this scene. As rocks pelt him, he gets on his knees. When I first began to study this passage I read several translations. One says that he fell to his knees. This caught my attention. I suppose that if a rock hit me in the head, I might fall to my knees, too. So I went to see my old friend, Dr. Strong, and looked it up in his concordance and dictionary. The phrase used in Acts 7 appears also in Acts 20, when Paul met with the elders from Ephesus and "he knelt down and prayed with them all."[7] The phrase also appears in Acts 9[8] when Peter knelt down beside the little girl's bed and raised her from the dead. The stones did not drive Stephen to his knees. He did what every knee shall do.

The Hebrew verb, *barak*, translated as "to bless", literally means to bend the knee. Stephen went to Hebrew school as a young boy. Every Jewish boy did. Although the New Testament was written in Greek, Stephen did not kneel in Greek. He knelt down in Hebrew. He knew what it meant. He knelt down to give a blessing.

Acts 7:60

Then he knelt down and cried out with a loud voice, "Lord, do not charge them with this sin." And when he had said this, he fell asleep.

Notice that he didn't whisper. He didn't whimper. He cried out with a loud voice. Forgiving and blessing are the cry of the victor, not the whimper of the victim. When someone has harmed us, we remain their victim until we forgive and bless them.

As I said earlier, we know of no one specifically that Stephen led to the Lord. But he did have one convert after he died. Stephen's death did not have an immediate effect on Saul, the young man holding the coats, but I believe that Jesus met Saul on the road to Damascus because of Stephen's blessing.

Consider this. As certainly the most often quoted book of the last two millennia, the Bible has had a greater impact on western civilization than any other single group of writings. This book, much more widely disseminated once the New Testament was added, has affected our societies and the way we govern our lives to this very day. This man, who later took the name of Paul, authored the largest portion of the New Testament, and you and I, in this very hour, participate in the blessing spoken by Stephen on the day he died almost two thousand years ago. This story demonstrates the power of blessing. When we bless, we speak God's intention, for He desires that all the nations of the earth be blessed. The blessings we speak today will endure through the generations and plot the future course of history.

The first words God ever spoke to man contained a blessing,[9] and the last verse of the Bible expresses a blessing.[10] As He ascended into heaven, in the last act of His earthly ministry, Jesus lifted up His hands and blessed His disciples.[11]

The Bible overflows with blessing, so it seems odd that we should know so little about how to do it. Having an enemy who works tirelessly to keep us oblivious of the power given to us could be part of the reason for our ignorance. The Devil cannot keep us from learning that blessings exist, so he tries to keep us confused with the notion that only God, or only a certain few, can function in the blessing business. Our own selfishness provides Satan with one of his favorite weapons in his warfare against us. We focus on ourselves, make mighty efforts to receive the Lord's blessing, and then, we will occasionally ask God to bless others when we are feeling generous.

Our past also hinders our efforts in learning how to bless. I sometimes minister in prisons, and many of the men I speak with feel that they have disqualified themselves from blessing their children because of their past failures. Often, sons and daughters refuse to forgive their fathers, and the fathers feel they have no right to speak into the lives of their children. But this is simply untrue. God has given every father and every mother the right, and even the responsibility, to bless their children.

Like a mighty river, blessing flows and the surest

way into that flow is to jump in. It doesn't matter if you don't know how to swim. The current will carry you along. It is not possible to drown. No matter how inept we feel, we cannot fail when we begin to bless.

Blessing vs. Praying

When we pray, we commune with God, so prayer takes many forms and expressions. When we pray, we can confess to God; we worship, praise, or give Him thanks; consecrate ourselves; or intercede for others. But the most common type of prayer takes the form of a petition, or a request. Paul succinctly describes this in Philippians 4:6:

> Be anxious for nothing, but in everything by prayer and supplication, with thanksgiving, let your requests be made known to God.

We can regard blessing as a form of prayer, too, but a blessing has some characteristics that set it distinctly apart from a prayer of petition. When we ask God to bless someone we pray, not bless. We do not give them our blessing; we ask Him to do it. Remember, we cannot do what only God can do, and God will not do what He has given us to do. Jesus didn't say, "Ask God to bless those who curse you." He said, "You bless those that curse you."

A petition seeks action from someone with power, authority, or means that we ourselves do not have. God has given to us the authority to bless. We do not need to ask Him for it; it already belongs to us.

My wife and I have spent long hours and many tears praying for our children and asking God to intervene when they fell into trouble or drifted from the Lord, but as we began blessing them, it became clear that blessing brings a greater effect. Please do not misunderstand. The prayer of petition is a powerful tool, but tools usually have specifically designed purposes. Asking God to bless someone is like using a pair of pliers to drive a railroad spike. It might work, but we need a sledge hammer, and the bigger the hammer, the better the blessing.

We can address God regarding the object of our blessing, or we can speak to that person directly. Whether he hears us or not has no significance in determining the effectiveness of our words. Notice that Stephen cried out to the Lord after he knelt down, but he did not make a request. He made a declaration, almost as if giving Jesus instructions; he said "Lord, do not lay this sin to their charge."

I think Jesus must have smiled when He heard Stephen echo the very words He Himself spoke while hanging on the cross, "Father, forgive them..."

While several examples occur in the Bible of people praying on their knees, remember that the very definition of the verb *to bless* requires the act of humbling ourselves signified by the bending of the knee. Not that we can't bless or pray standing up, but our inner posture indicates a difference between the two. The inner posture, or attitude, of a petition seeks to receive, while the attitude of a blessing seeks to give. Jesus and Stephen both, at the moment of their greatest affliction, did not request forgiveness for their persecutors but granted them full pardon. They each moved from victim to victor by speaking a blessing.

In light of the Hebrew definition for blessing, I find this verse fascinating.

Hebrews 7:7

Now beyond all contradiction the lesser is blessed by the better.

Beyond question, the greater blesses the lesser, and yet, in blessing, the greater must bend the knee in humility. Jesus' life displays authority clothed in humility, and when we bless, we can do so with full confidence knowing that as sure as God gives grace to the humble,[12] our words are authorized by God Himself.

Diction, or our choice of words, marks a second contrast between a prayer and a blessing. Blessings often contain the word *may*. Look at one of my favorite examples:

Psalms 20:1-4

1 May the Lord answer you in the day of trouble; may the name of the God of Jacob defend you;

2 May He send you help from the sanctuary, and strengthen you out of Zion;

3 May He remember all your offerings, and accept your burnt sacrifice.

4 May He grant you according to your heart's desire, and fulfill all your purpose.

I don't suggest that you have to speak in an exact form; blessing has no room for legalism, and it's more an art than a science. Simple practice will make you more comfortable and confident, and confidence will bring limitless possibilities. You can bless anything that lies within your arena of responsibility. In other words, you can bless anything in your life, including anyone who may have ill intentions toward you.

The best advice I could give anyone who wishes to begin to learn how to bless would be this: Blessing does not think about receiving anything. It is all about giving and is probably the godliest characteristic we can have. So when blessing, don't think "ask;" think "give."[13]

Forgiveness is not an occasional act: it is an attitude.

Martin Luther King Jr.

Questions
and Objections

I love questions and even objections, as both allow me to clarify a point, remember something I've forgotten to say, or think about a new perspective. I find that most people learn from and appreciate these things too, and since we are not face-to-face, I have included a few comments and questions that I've received in hopes of answering some things I may have missed.

I do not have unforgiveness.

If anyone has spent time in Christian circles, most likely they have heard a message on forgiveness at some point and know that they should forgive. Many tell me they do not have forgiveness issues, and they have forgiven everyone who has ever wronged them. However, just because we don't remember an incident or offense doesn't mean we don't have hidden issues. In fact, I've found that people who say they have absolutely no one they need to forgive usually have someone they need to forgive. It's better to say that we don't know of anyone, than to say there isn't anyone.

I routinely speak on forgiveness in a variety of settings. In one instance, I conducted workshops over several days with the members of a south Texas congregation. A woman in one of the seminars emphatically said that she had forgiven everyone in her life. I suggested that she ask the Lord if she had any unforgiveness. After all, if anyone knew it would be Him. She said she would, but she knew for certain that she had no issues. Although the woman traveled out of town that weekend, she sent a message to me Sunday morning through one of her friends. "She discovered that she had taken up an offense against her son-in-law" the friend said, "because of the way he had treated her daughter." The mother-in-law had found a way to be gracious to her son-in-law in order to cope with the situation, but coping is not forgiving. Coping provides a way to live and work around issues. It does not resolve them. Coping can make it appear as though we have forgiven, but we can only know for certain by asking the Lord to convict us of any unforgiveness we might have.

Accepting His list, and not making one of our own, should follow the first step of asking God to convict us. Remember the young man whose mother abandoned him at age eleven? The Lord started him with the lesser hurt caused by his roommate. He may have had large and long-standing mother issues, but in this case, they took a backseat to a more immediate offense. Forgiving takes faith, but believing for the big things often overwhelms us. Thank God we can start with the not so big. Gaining small, but increasing victories gives us confidence to face the big battles. We must ask God to look at our hearts and drop all assumptions about what He might say to us. We will surely misconstrue His instructions if we assume we know them already. He always accepts us where we are and as we are, and if we are willing to begin, He will take us to where He wants us to be.

When folks insistently tell me that they have no unforgiveness, I don't challenge them. I don't usually believe them, either, but I don't know their hearts. Only God does. So I ask them a question. "If you have forgiven everyone you need to, have you blessed them?" Usually they admit that they haven't. Forgiving equals only half of forgiveness; it takes blessing to complete it and make it stick.

I will forgive them, but they have to ask me.

This sounds pretty good, and some folks feel they have scripture to back it up, but consider this: Did God forgive us before or after we asked? Jesus is the Lamb, slain before the foundation of the world. God provided forgiveness for us long before we became aware we even needed it. Occasionally, we take up an offense when the offender never intended to harm us. Sometimes we can even imagine slights and insult where none exist. That person doesn't know he has offended us, and therefore doesn't know to ask for forgiveness. Should I hold this unforgiveness, reaping its bitter end, while I wait for him to come to me? Sounds a little like pride.

What about forgiving God?

Such a great question. A perfect God never does anything wrong, then why, or how, can we forgive Him?

We must remember that forgiveness concerns us more than the one we forgive. When we forgive God we simply release any offense we may have taken up against Him, and then we may say with the psalmist, "I will bless the Lord at all times. His praise shall continually be in my mouth."[1]

I meet many super-spiritual Christians who say that God has never offended them. I used to say that myself. But the Lord has many times done things that I didn't like and that have often angered me: things I didn't understand, things that cost me greatly. It has taken a long time for me to come to terms with some of those things. To say, "His ways are not my ways, and God is always right," has never worked for me. But as I worked those things out with the Lord, as I wrestled with Him, the whats and the whys became so much less important because I began to know His heart. I always wanted that anyway, in spite of what it has or might cost me.

When the Lord doesn't meet our expectations we may easily take up an offense against Him, because we feel that He disappointed us. Horribly abused and greatly wounded, many say, "Where was God? He had the power to stop this from happening to me, but He didn't do it. He abandoned me in my most desperate hour." He was there, as He is here now. He loved you then, and He loves you now. He offers His heart to you. You shall have it, if you will embrace Him, and begin to forgive and bless those who have harmed you.

I can't forgive myself.

When I began to study forgiveness, I experienced difficulty with forgiving myself. It seemed like I was excusing what I'd done and letting myself off the hook. As I prayed and thought about it, I came to the conclusion that forgiving myself really means nothing more than accepting God's forgiveness. After talking with hundreds of people,

I believe that I have discovered two reasons why we cannot receive God's forgiveness and thereby forgive ourselves:

•Having unforgiveness toward someone else prevents us from experiencing God's forgiveness. In Matthew 6 Jesus taught His disciples to pray, and gave them the model prayer.

> Our Father in heaven, Hallowed be Your name.
>
> Your kingdom come, Your will be done, on earth as it is in heaven.
>
> Give us this day our daily bread.
>
> And forgive us our debts, as we forgive our debtors.
>
> And do not lead us into temptation, but deliver us from the evil one.
>
> For Yours is the kingdom and the power and the glory forever. Amen.[2]

As one of the most famous passages from the scripture, these few verses have generated tens of thousands, if not millions, of sermons. Yet Jesus himself commented on only one thought. He didn't speak of the power or the glory, or even of the kingdom to come. He had only one thing to say. "For if you forgive men their trespasses, your heavenly Father will also forgive you. But if you do not forgive men their trespasses, neither will your Father forgive your trespasses."[3] Simply and directly, He instructs that if we do not forgive, we will not be forgiven. Many many Christians battle guilt and condemnation, suffer torment, and do not have the peace that comes from knowing without a doubt that their sins are fully and finally forgiven. As we discovered in the Terrible Parable, God reinstates our debt when we will not forgive. Any unforgiveness makes us incapable of receiving and walking in the forgiveness that Jesus purchased for us at Calvary. We forfeit the forgiveness we have in Christ when we choose to not forgive others.

•Pride will also prevent us from receiving God's forgiveness. When we do foolish or hurtful things and then realize what we have done, we usually begin to beat ourselves up. "I know better than that," we say. Or, "How could I have acted so foolishly?" These blunders violate the image we have constructed of ourselves, and in our minds, we consider them inexcusable. We become disillusioned with ourselves. Someone once said that God can never be disillusioned with us, because He never had any illusions about us in the first place. When we act as if we have sinned beyond forgiveness, we hold ourselves to a higher standard than God does. In essence, we say that Jesus died for all sin, but mine is the exception. Such thinking says that almighty God cannot forgive us and declares our sin as more powerful than Him. We may not have this conscious intention, but holding these thoughts catapults us beyond mere pride to arrogance of the highest order.

I have a right not to forgive.

Yes, you do have that right, but can you afford to exercise it? In every way, unforgiveness exacts an extreme cost. Like an armed robber, it strangles the future and leaves us without hope. And the Devil, too, has a right to torment us if we choose to not forgive.[4]

They don't deserve to be forgiven.

No, they don't. And neither do we. Mercy does not come to the worthy or deserving. If they deserved it, forgiveness wouldn't be necessary. Forgiveness is for those things which cannot be made right. Those who say that others don't deserve to be forgiven usually don't believe they deserve to be forgiven themselves and often have difficulty trusting God. On one hand they play God, and on the other, they don't know Him. It seems our view of God is often reflected in how we treat others.

I've tried, but I can't forgive.

Those who say this have often given up after making an honest effort, but they usually haven't begun to bless the one they desire to forgive. Staying on the merry-go-round and never getting past zero will frustrate and dishearten anyone. The act of blessing actually requires much less effort than cycling back and forth between forgiving and trying to stay at zero.

I'll forgive them someday, but I'm not ready now.

If you wait until you think you're ready, it will never happen. If you are born again, then you are born ready to forgive.

It's not genuine unless I really feel like forgiving.

He who trusts in his own heart is a fool, but whoever walks wisely will be delivered (Proverbs 28:26). Remember, emotions give us lagging indicators. Forgiveness begins with a decision, and we can make that decision regardless of how we feel. Our choice determines authenticity, not our feelings, and that holds true for both forgiving and blessing.

What if the person I need to forgive and bless is dead?

We can forgive anybody for anything, anytime, and alive or dead doesn't matter. The same goes for blessing. I once met a man who had spent most of his adult life in prison for manslaughter. Even while incarcerated he had killed two other men. A large man, his face bore the scars of the life he had lived. When he was ten years old his father, in a drunken rage, broke several of his bones and beat him until he lost consciousness. At that young age, he vowed to kill his father. In bar fights and brawls he exacted from others the revenge he wanted from his father. Eventually, the brutality he experienced as a child, and the murder he had sown in his heart, came to full fruition when he killed a man with his bare hands.

I marveled when he confessed that he had hated his father even more because his father had died before he could kill him. But he also confessed he knew that this hatred had destroyed his life. He had no excuses for what he had done, and I could see that something had gone out of him. As I led him through a declaration of forgiveness, I watched him let his anger go, and we gave this blessing to his deceased father: "May God, the One who has the power to work everything for good, use this man's life to turn many to the Lord. May his sons be men of peace. May they be kind fathers and gentle husbands. May all his children, and all his children's children reap a harvest of righteousness, peace and joy." This might be a little hard to understand, but someone who has passed on is not really dead, at least in the sense that they have ceased to exist. In death, that passage from the earthly to the eternal realm, everyone leaves something behind. They remain in the memory of those who knew them. Their actions affected many, both directly and indirectly, and very often children and other family members survive them.

We must remember Joseph's testimony. His brothers had sold him as a slave and told his father that a wild animal had killed him. He lost his family and everything he held dear. When he finally met his brothers many years later, he could say to them, "You meant it for evil, but God meant it for good, to save the lives of many."[5] God's great redemptive power can bring something brilliant and noble and magnificent out of the most horrific and gruesome violations. The scripture says, "He gives us beauty for ashes, and the oil of joy for mourning."[6]

Should I forgive or bless them in person?

Since forgiveness concerns us first, and the offending party second, I usually advise people not to go to the person right away. It usually sounds condescending to say to someone, "I forgive you." Give it time.

A young college student came to one of our seminars with his girlfriend's parents. He had been sleeping on their couch because his mother had disinherited him after his father's recent death. She had cut off all of his funding and wouldn't speak with him. He had no place to live, and no money for next semester's tuition. If he knew, he didn't say why she had done this, and we didn't probe. He simply forgave and blessed her as we had taught, and we later learned that she called him the very next morning and wanted to see him. We have hundreds of testimonies from those who have forgiven and blessed someone and then received an unexpected call from that person within a matter of days, or even hours. Since forgiveness operates in the realm of the spirit, time and space cannot restrict it. If we will forgive and bless before meeting our offender face to face or on the telephone, we can speak with them in genuine humility and honesty when the opportunity comes.

I'll forgive them but I'll never trust them.

Forgiveness, reconciliation, and trust are all separate issues. Once trust has been violated, it is not easily restored. Forgiveness can be granted, but trust must be earned. A battered wife, for example, should forgive her husband, but forgiving him doesn't mean that she has to put herself in harm's way. Forgiveness makes it possible to re-establish trust, but doesn't guarantee it.

If we don't have forgiveness, then we don't have anything.

Robert Shackelford

My Story

At the first of this book, I briefly mentioned discovering the missing element of blessing when my understanding of forgiveness at that time had failed me. To give greater context to this discovery, here's my story.

I first met Bob while in my mid-twenties. As a retired Air Force sergeant in his forties and an impressive figure at six foot four or so, his bearing seemed imposing at first glance. A second look though, or even a word from him, revealed a man with open arms and an open heart. He had an admirable transparency oddly accompanied by a brusque manner. I didn't know if he was a teddy bear or a drill sergeant, but I knew I just wanted to stand beside him.

Bob had taken a personal and pastoral interest in me, and in the spring of the next year, I moved to the town where he lived and began to travel with him in his ministry. In those days most of spiritual life revolved around traditional congregations, but God had put a hunger in the hearts of many people, and they had begun to gather in homes to pray, to worship, and to hear Bible teaching. Bob ministered in several of these home meetings during the week, and on the weekend, I would drive him to the larger towns and cities where he spoke in more traditional church settings.

Most of what I know about "the ministry" I learned from Bob as we drove the highways of north central Texas. He was the first man I had met who could see the Church as something greater than an organization. I never did learn how to pastor a church in the traditional sense, but I did learn how to pastor people and to lead by example. I also learned how to relate to the Lord.

On one occasion we arrived a few minutes before meeting time during a summer thunderstorm. I don't think we had an umbrella, and as the rain came down in buckets, I began to gather up Bibles and notebooks and prepare myself for a mad dash to the door. "Wait," Bob said. "God will stop the rain."

"What?" I replied.

"God will stop the rain."

"I don't need Him to stop the rain," I said.

"Just wait," he responded. "The Lord wants to show you something. He cares for you even when you think you don't need Him to."

Sure enough, in about four or five minutes, the rain stopped, and we took our leisure getting into the building. A couple of minutes after we entered, the rain began to fall again, and for the next two and a half hours we spent in that building, I could hear the torrent beating against the windows. By the time we started out the door at the end of the meeting, the rain had stopped. It resumed as soon as I started the car and rained heavily on us while we drove ten minutes to a restaurant for pie and coffee. When we pulled into the parking lot, it stopped again, started again once we were inside, and stopped when we were ready to leave. It rained once more while we drove to our hotel and stopped again so we could safely and dryly enter. The next day the storm passed and the skies cleared.

You may or may not believe this story. No matter, I was there and saw it happen. I don't know if the Lord did that for him or for me, or for both of us, but I did learn that I could set aside my hasty eagerness, have just a little patience, and give God an opportunity to move — a lesson that has served me well over the years.

Bob once told me that observing how small children respond to you could indicate your general spiritual condition, and if they consistently reacted negatively or fearfully to you in normal settings, you probably had something going on that you needed to ask the Lord about.

He loved to ask his favorite question, "What's the Lord saying to you?" Those who knew him learned to have a ready answer, especially if they hadn't seen him in a few days. That question always heightened our awareness that God wants to have a continual conversation with us. He once asked it of a five year old boy. Imagine a six-and-a-half-footer towering over a three-footer. The little man cocked his head to one side, thought for a moment and seriously said, "Play more; eat more ice cream."

Bob just smiled and said, "I believe you've heard the Lord."

By the time I came along, Bob had already taken a few men under his wing, and as his influence began to grow more and more came to him. Twelve years later that influence had spread internationally and his ministry had grown considerably. He had promoted me into several leadership positions, and I had become a key figure in the local operations, overseeing many endeavors. He had high expectations; I had problems saying no, and I soon became overloaded. It seemed as though I had three or four full time jobs. Not a detail man himself, Bob needed detail men to serve under him. As I found myself responsible for so many people, things, and areas of ministry, my lack of talent for detail soon became apparent.

One day he called me into his office and told me he had given all of my responsibilities to someone else. Completely disenfranchised in one moment,

I suddenly had nothing. If I could be stripped of it so easily, then what I had worked and sacrificed for was only an illusion. I think that realization hurt the most.

With the clarity of hindsight, I understand now that this event merely culminated a series of events. I had spread myself so thinly that I had become ineffective in almost every area of my life. But most of all, I had allowed what God had called me to do to displace who God had called me to be. I had made my own personal relationship with the Lord second place to my ministry.

Still, I felt betrayed. Rejection seared me like a hard, hot west Texas wind blowing sand in my face, and at times it felt so physically real that I would lift my hands in front of my eyes and turn my head to ease the pain. Hurt and wounded, I first thought of retaliation, but somehow I knew that the Lord did not want me to defend or justify myself. I could have caused great turmoil among the churches and fellowships in our sphere of influence, but that one little bit of restraint saved me and many others from much grief. Left with fight or flight, I could do neither. So I withdrew and lost myself in 90 hour construction work weeks. But in my emotional and physical exhaustion, the Lord began to visit me and bring the scripture to mind. I thought about John 20:23 where *forgive* is translated as *remit* in the KJV. This brought to mind Romans 8:32 which says that God delivered up Jesus for our offenses and freely gave us all things when He raised Him from the dead. Somehow I caught this simple concept — that forgiving gets you to zero and blessing gets you past it — and I began to apply it. I can't say that I recovered overnight, but the process was sure.

In many ways, this man who became my father in the Lord resembled my natural father. Both men, while relatively young, lost a parent, and both escaped the harshness of farm life by joining the military. Both of them fell victim to the pressures of that world, and both had father issues they needed to resolve. But unlike my father, this man came to walk with the Lord well before the end of his life. The Lord afforded me the opportunity to work out many of my own father issues in my relationship with Bob. This stripping had caused me to feel rejected. In turn I wanted to reject the years I had spent with him and count them as worthless and wasted, just as I had done with my natural dad. Forgiving and blessing brought redemption — and appreciation.

As I grew older, I began to understand the personal cost of leadership and that leading men to discover their destinies in God requires a greater price than leading mere organizations. A jar of clay can hold a heavenly treasure, but youths often stumble over these earthen vessels and in their need and rebellion abandon the riches within. God uses men with weakness so that His power and glory are unmistakable. A wise man knows how to mine the treasure, and honor the vessel without making too much of it one way or the other. Or as Bob used to say in his down home way, "We ought to be as smart as cows. A cow will chew up the grass and spit out the sticks."

As the years passed, we restored our relationship, but I never asked Bob why he did it. By the time I came to the place where I could ask him such a question, I no longer needed to know the answer. God in His sovereignty had arranged a Gethsemane for me, and there I discovered what was important and what was not. At the end of Bob's life, I was privileged to stand beside his hospital bed with his wife and several of his children. As all the monitors flat-lined and as he passed into eternity, the tears rolled down my cheeks, and I could say, "Thank you." Thank you to him, thank you to my dad-- by then dead for many years — and thank You to my Father in heaven. I knew that none of the sticks really mattered.

That's how I learned to fully forgive. The lesson cost me dearly but has proved a small price to pay.

The Book
of Blessings

**May the Lord increase you
a thousand fold, and bless
you as He has promised.**

Deuteronomy 1:11

How to Use the List

CERTAINLY, BY THIS POINT in the book, you have thought of someone you need to forgive. I cannot overstate the importance of putting into practice what you have learned as soon as possible. Forgiving and blessing should become a lifestyle, not an occasional event. Fortunately, we only need three things to incorporate them into our daily lives: practice, practice, practice. At first, you may feel uncomfortable with the idea of blessing, but after trying it half a dozen times, it comes easily. At this point, I hope you see the value of making blessing a regular part of your life. You can eventually deal with all of your old forgiveness issues, quickly remedy any new ones, and make blessing a lifelong activity.

In this section I have included example blessings for some common offenses and celebratory occasions, a model for a declaration of forgiveness, and lastly a list of 1001 blessings. While by no means exhaustive, this list can serve as a handbook and provide a way for you to begin to compose your own blessings. I have paraphrased all of the blessings on the list from the Scripture, so please, do not feel bound to state them exactly the way I have. Adapt any of it to suit your needs. Ask the Lord to teach you how to bless, and then you can take ownership of the process for yourself. The most important thing is just to do it, and do it now.

Initially, I had hoped to categorize this list of blessings in an effort to make it user friendly. The task proved impossible. Some of them fit neatly into a category, but most defied classification and fit into several groups. In the end I decided to simply number them and include an index. Browse the list and begin. Put your blessings in writing. You may also choose to write them on an index card, take it with you, and read it out loud from time to time. I know you will find good success.

Starting Points

The simplest way to compose a blessing is to simply pick some characteristics from the listings in the index, choose a few blessings under each heading and then put them together. If you would like to bless someone with peace, health and prosperity, pick three blessings under peace, two each from health and prosperity, and there, in no time at all, you have a seven-fold blessing. If you don't know which categories to choose, here are some starting points.

Blessing Oppositely to the Offense

To compose a blessing I usually use one of four starting points. The first involves blessing the person opposite to the way they have offended me. I try to liken the blessing to the nature of the offense. If someone tries to cheat me out of some money, I will bless them with financial prosperity and sometimes even send them an offering. If someone has spoken ill of me, I will begin to speak well of them.

The four most common types of offenses include rejection, abandonment, abuse, and betrayal. All four of these are connected and intertwined. A child who has been abandoned by a parent may also feel rejected and blame himself for that parent's absence. Someone who feels rejected will usually also feel like a reject, worthless or of very little value. Victims of abuse also feel some form of rejection, and abuse itself is often a betrayal; betrayal can only result when we have first trusted someone.

Security and safety, acceptance and value, and favor and affirmation oppose rejection and the feeling of worthlessness it engenders. Here are a few blessings from the list:

> 84. May the Lord arise and set you in safety.

> 482. May you dwell in the secret place of the Most High and abide under the shadow of the Almighty.

> 488. May He calm the storm so that its waves are still and may He guide you to your desired haven.

> 99. May he hide you in the time of trouble and set your feet upon the Rock.

> 156. May He lead you safely so that you do not fear.

> 79. May you sleep in peace and dwell in safety.

> 249. May you hearken unto the voice of wisdom, dwell safely and be quiet from fear of evil.

> 369. May you know Him who says, "I will never leave you nor forsake you."

> 77. May the Lord lift up the light of His countenance upon you.

> 144. May the Lord daily load you with benefits.

> 189. May you know that God is for you.

> 855. May you find favor and good understanding in the sight of God and

man.

986. May the Lord count you worthy of
His calling, and fulfill all the good pleasure
of His goodness and the work of faith with
power.

658. May you be counted worthy of
double honor.

890. May you walk worthy of the Lord,
fully pleasing Him, being fruitful in every
good work and increasing in the knowledge
of God.

For this example I have chosen fifteen blessings
from the list. I won't use them all, but will reduce
this number to three or four or so, and then
compose my blessing. Let's use 99, 156, 79, 369,
and 855. Here's our new list:

99. May He hide you in the time of trouble
and set your feet upon the Rock.

156. May He lead you safely so that you
do not fear.

79. May you sleep in peace and dwell in
safety.

369. May you know Him who says, "I will
never leave you nor forsake you."

855. May you find favor and good
understanding in the sight of God and
man.

I really like 189, too, so I think I'll start with
it. Now, our composed blessing for the miscreant
who has rejected us:

"May you know that the Lord is for you,
and may He hide you from trouble. May
you live free from fear, sleep in peace and
dwell in safety. May you know that He will

never leave you nor forsake you, and may you find favor with God and man. May you walk worthy of the Lord, fully pleasing Him, being fruitful in every good work."

Notice that I added 890. Once I start blessing it's hard to stop. This simple process becomes very easy to master. Collect some blessings from the list and use them as thoughts to compose your own blessing. As you read the scripture you will no doubt find many other blessings that you can put to good use.

Let's try another one. The opposite of betrayal is faithfulness, so here's a collection for that:

> 655. May the Lord enable you to do His will, and may He count you faithful.
>
> 570. May you be faithful and abound with blessings.
>
> 579. May you not waver at the promise of God, but be strengthened in faith, and be fully convinced that what He had promised He was also able to perform.

This list seems to flow together, so I'll use them just as we find them with only a slight change.

> "May the Lord enable you to do His will. May He count you faithful, and may you abound with blessings. May you not waver at the promise of God, but be strengthened in faith, and be fully convinced that what He has promised He is also able to perform."

Blessing for Something Needed or Missing

The second starting point includes blessing for something needed or missing. People often offend us simply because they are afraid — afraid of loss, afraid of failure, afraid of rejection, or afraid of not getting what they need. Since perfect love casts out fear, then love will provide freedom. This would bless someone battling fear, and uses 617:

> "May they know the love of Christ, which passes knowledge, and may they be so secure in His love for them, that nothing can disturb them."

Sometimes people need to repent, but I never bless them with repentance for anything specific. Since I can only see the outer things and not their heart, blessings like that can very easily turn into a judgment which actually works against blessing. Since the goodness, or kindness, of God leads us to repentance, a blessing for those who need to change their ways might look like this:

> "May the Lord show you His kindness and the richness of His grace, and may goodness and mercy follow you all the days of your life."

This is a really good blessing whether they need to repent or not. You may want that one for yourself. It makes use of 448 and 884.

The Golden Rule Blessing

The third starting point simply embraces the golden rule. "Do unto others as you would have them do unto you." If I can't get started with either of the other two, I will bless them like I want to be blessed myself. Sometimes I don't feel right about someone, but I don't know why. They may irritate me in some small way, or just simply seem indifferent or rude. Often service persons — waiters, clerks and attendants — act in this way. I will try to imagine what it is like to have their job, think about how I want to be treated as a customer and fill my conversation with them with appropriate blessings. It amazes me how often and how quickly their attitudes will change.

Ceremonial Blessings: Blessing the Future

Our last starting point considers the future. I perform a few weddings from time to time, and I like to incorporate a blessing for the bride and groom into the service. Whenever possible, I like to have the fathers of the couple speak their blessings as part of the ceremony. Here are some actual blessings that I have used in weddings.

Father of the bride to the groom

May you live joyfully all the days of your life with the wife of your youth, and may you always be enraptured with her love. May you be a faithful man who walks in integrity, and may your children be blessed after you. May the Lord give you wisdom and teach you to trust and fear Him. And may you love your wife like Christ loves the church.

Father of the groom to the bride

May the heart of your husband safely trust in you. May you do him good all of the days of your life. May you be adorned with the hidden person of the heart, with the incorruptible beauty of a gentle and quiet spirit, which is very precious in the sight of God. May strength and honor be your clothing and may you rejoice in the future.

Father of the bride to the couple

May the Lord lift up the light of His countenance upon you. May He put gladness in your hearts, and may you sleep in peace and dwell in safety. May you love one another fervently with a pure heart. May the Lord preserve you, and may you see His goodness in the land of the living. May you never waver at the promise of God, but be strengthened in faith, and be fully convinced that what He has promised, He is also able to perform. May the Lord enrich you in everything and in every way.

Father of the groom to the couple

May the Lord fill your mouth with laughter and your tongue with singing. May your hearts be pure, and your words pleasant. May God give you strength, bless you with peace, and in health and vigor may you live out every day allotted to you. May you see the goodness of the Lord in the land of the living. Now may the God of hope fill you with all joy and peace in believing, that you may abound in hope by the power of the Holy Spirit. And may you be fruitful and multiply.

Other occasions for blessings of this type include coming of age ceremonies, graduations, or the launch of any type of new venture.

So, dear reader, as we come to the end of this brief missive on forgiveness, I want to thank you for your time and attention, and here is my blessing for you:

May the word of God richly dwell in you. May it be a light to your path and a lamp for your feet. May it be the joy and the rejoicing of your heart, and may you always be a doer of the word. May the Lord delight in you, and may you see His goodness in the land of the living. May you live out every day allotted to you in health and vigor. May the Lord fulfill all of your purpose. May the meditation of your heart always be pleasing to Him, and may you know Him like He knows you. May the Lord teach you how to bless, and may you be known as one who is mighty in blessing. And may this proverb be true of you: "The blessing of the Lord makes rich in every way, and He adds no sorrow to it."

One last thing—you don't have to wait for someone to offend you before you can give them a blessing. You can bless anyone, anytime, for any reason.

Declaration of Forgiveness

When making this declaration of forgiveness, put the person's name and offense(s) in the appropriate blanks. Then choose two or three blessings from the list and tailor them for the person you are blessing. Speak them out. It is important to say all of this out loud. Remember, blessing is an act of transfer through word or action. Just thinking a blessing does not qualify as blessing someone. At the very least, blessings must be spoken. Occasionally substitute their name for the pronoun you. Start small. Keep it simple. You'll be amazed at what happens, and you'll be an expert in blessing in no time.

Model for the act of forgiveness:

Father, I thank You that Jesus paid for all of my sins when He died on the cross, and that You have granted me total forgiveness. Because You have forgiven me, I now, of my own free will, choose to forgive _____ for _____. Do not lay this sin to their charge. No matter what else they have done, do not hold this sin against them. Here is my blessing for them…

The List

The List

1. **M**ay God set you in a family.

2. **M**ay you live out your full days and may your descendants be established before Him.

3. **M**ay God make your descendants mighty on the earth.

4. **M**ay God grant the barren woman a home like a joyful mother of children.

5. **M**ay the Lord give you increase more and more, you and your children.

6. **M**ay the Lord build your house and guard your city.

7. **M**ay the Lord give you children as your heritage from Him.

8. **M**ay your children be like arrows in the hand of a mighty man.

9. **M**ay your wife be like a fruitful vine and your children like olive plants.

10. **M**ay you dwell together in unity.

11. **M**ay your sons be as plants grown up in their youth and your daughters be pillars sculptured in palatial style.

12. **M**ay the Lord bless your home.

13. **M**ay you hear the instruction of a father and gain understanding.

14. **M**ay your heart retain your father's words and keep his commandments that you may live.

15. **M**ay you rejoice with the wife of your youth. May you always be enraptured with her love.

16. **M**ay you find life and obtain favor from the Lord.

17. May your father's commandment and the law of your mother lead you and keep you when you sleep. May their commandments be a lamp and the law a light.

18. May you be wise and make your father glad and may righteousness deliver you from death.

19. May your thoughts be righteous and may your house stand.

20. May you be an excellent wife, the crown of your husband.

21. May you choose your friends carefully.

22. May you be wise and hear your father's instruction.

23. May you be a good man and leave an inheritance to your children.

24. May you have the strong confidence of the fear of the Lord.

25. May your children have a place of refuge.

26. May your home be filled with quietness.

27. May you find a wife and obtain favor from the Lord.

28. May you have a prudent wife.

29. May you have a prudent husband.

30. May you be a faithful man who walks in integrity.

31. May you bless your father and mother, and may the Lord teach you how to honor them.

32. May you have a good name and the loving favor of the Lord.

33. May you train up your children in the way they should go.

34. May your father and mother rejoice that they have a wise child.

35. May you love wisdom and cause your father to rejoice.

36. May the heart of your husband safely trust in you.

37. May you do your husband good, and not evil, all the days of your life.

38. May you love your wife like Christ loves the church.

39. May your husband be known in the gates and sit among the elders.

40. May your children rise up and call you blessed, and may your husband praise you.

41. May you live joyfully all the days of your life with the wife whom you love.

42. May you be perfectly joined together in the same mind and in the same judgment.

43. May you bring up your children in the nurture and admonition of the Lord.

44. May you know how to serve as a son.

45. May the Lord grant mercy to your household, and may He often refresh you.

46. May your children be blessed, and may they have a bright hope and a future.

47. May you love one another fervently with a pure heart.

48. May you give honor to your wife, as your coheir of the grace of life, and may your prayers be unhindered.

49. May you bless the Lord with a heart that is whole. May you see and tell of all His marvelous works.

50. May He strengthen your heart.

51. May the Lord be your strength and your shield and bless you with peace.

52. May the Lord heal you, and keep you alive.

53. May you live long and see many good days.

54. May you know that the Lord is near to you and will deliver you out of all your afflictions.

55. May the Lord preserve you in safety and keep you alive.

56. May the Lord strengthen you and sustain you.

57. May the Lord be merciful to you and raise you up.

58. May the Lord restore you.

59. May God place His hand upon you and make you strong.

60. May God preserve your life.

61. May God satisfy you with long life and His salvation.

62. May you bear fruit in old age and be fresh and flourishing.

63. May the comforts of the Lord delight your soul.

64. May God forgive you all your iniquities and heal all your diseases.

65. May God renew your youth like the eagle's.

66. May God uphold you according to His word that you may live and not be ashamed of your hope.

67. May God's tender mercies come to you that you may live.

68. May the Lord give you sleep.

69. May the Lord heal your broken heart and bind up your wounds.

70. May the Lord lengthen your days and give you hope and gladness.

71. May you have a sound heart.

72. May you have a merry heart and a cheerful countenance.

73. May you live many years
and rejoice in them all.

74. May your heart
be comforted

75. May the Spirit of Him who raised
Jesus from the dead quicken
your mortal body.

76. May you be like Moses, whose eye
was not dim and whose steps
did not falter all the days
of His life.

77. May the Lord lift up the light
of His countenance upon you.

78. May He put gladness
in your heart.

79. May you sleep in peace
and dwell in safety.

80. May you shout for joy because
the Lord is your defender.

81. May His favor surround
you like a shield.

82. May the Lord be your refuge
in time of trouble.

83. May the Lord remember you
and fulfill your expectation.

84. May the Lord arise and
set you in safety.

85. May you put your trust in the Lord, and may He preserve you.

86. May He be your portion and maintain that which He has allotted to you.

87. May you take pleasure in your inheritance.

88. May your lips be pure and your mouth without transgression.

89. May he uphold you in His path that your footsteps do not slip.

90. May the Lord answer you in the day of trouble.

91. May His name defend you and set you on high.

92. May He send you help and strengthen you.

93. May He remember all of your offerings and accept your burnt sacrifices.

94. May the Lord deliver you when you cry to Him, and may you not be put to shame.

95. May He lead you to still waters, and make you lie down in green pastures.

96. May the Lord anoint you, and may your cup run over.

97. May the Lord bring you out of all your distresses.

98. May the Lord redeem you out of all your troubles.

99. May he hide you in the time of trouble and set your feet upon the Rock.

100. May the Lord have mercy on you and hear your cry.

101. May you be of good courage and wait on the Lord.

102. May your heart greatly rejoice and may your mouth be filled with songs of praise.

103. May the Lord be your strength and saving refuge.

104. May you know the voice of the Lord.

105. May the Lord strengthen your heart so that you may be of good courage.

106. May the Lord be your hiding place and surround you with songs of deliverance.

107. May the Lord instruct you and teach you in the way you should go.

108. May the Lord put into your hand that which He has stored up for you.

109. May you hear the Lord singing over you with joy.

110. May you sing to Him a new song.

111. May you know that the earth is full of the goodness of the Lord.

112. May you stand in awe of Him.

113. May the Lord help you and be your shield.

114. May your heart rejoice in Him and may you trust in His name.

115. May you bless the Lord at all times. May His praise continually be in your mouth.

116. May you look to Him and be radiant.

117. May the Lord deliver you from all your fears.

118. May the angel of the Lord encamp around you, and deliver you.

119. May you taste and see that the Lord is good.

120. May the Lord teach you to fear Him.

121. May you keep your tongue from evil and your lips from speaking deceit.

122. May you seek peace and pursue it.

123. May you know that none who trust in the Lord will be condemned.

124. May the Lord plead your cause, be your protector and shield, and stand up for you.

125. May the Lord stop those that pursue you.

126. May your soul be joyful in the Lord, and may you rejoice in His salvation.

127. May you dwell in the land, and feed on His faithfulness.

128. May you be blessed on the earth.

129. May His countenance be your help.

130. May the Lord send out His light and His truth to lead you.

131. May He sustain you and never permit you to be moved.

132. May you not fear what flesh can do to you.

133. May God be merciful to you.

134. May your heart be steadfast.

135. May you sing and give praise.

136. May the Lord shelter you.

137. May you dwell in the tabernacle of the Lord forever and ever.

138. May you sing praise to the Lord forever and perform your vows to Him.

139. May the Lord be your rock and your salvation and your defense and your glory.

140. May the Lord be your refuge.

141. May your soul be satisfied with marrow and fatness.

142. May His right hand uphold you.

143. May God be merciful to you and bless you and cause His face to shine upon you.

144. May the Lord daily load you with benefits.

145. May the Lord deliver you
out of the mire.

146. May the Lord be your strong
refuge, your rock and
your fortress.

147. May God be your
hope and trust.

148. May God be close to you
and make haste to help you.

149. May God revive you and bring
you up from the depths
of the earth.

150. May God deliver you
when you cry.

151. May God redeem your life
from oppression and violence.

152. May God remind you of
His promises and mercy.

153. May you remember the years of
the right hand of the
Most High.

154. May God lead
you like a flock.

155. May you remember
His power.

156. May He lead you safely
so that you do not fear.

157. May God shepherd you according to the integrity of His heart and guide you by the skillfulness of His hands.

158. May God's tender mercies come speedily to meet you.

159. May God prepare room for you and cause you to take deep root.

160. May the Lord make His footsteps your pathway.

161. May God show you a sign for good.

162. May all your springs be in Him.

163. May you rejoice in the name of the Lord.

164. May God satisfy you early with His mercy that you may rejoice and be glad all your days.

165. May the beauty of the Lord be upon you.

166. May God deliver you from the snare of the fowler and the perilous pestilence.

167. May God cover you with His feathers and give you refuge under His wings.

168. May God's truth be your shield and buckler.

169. May the Lord be to you "God-Who-Forgives."

170. May you enter into His gates with thanksgiving and into His courts with praise.

171. May you sing of mercy and justice.

172. May you behave wisely in a perfect way.

173. May you set nothing wicked before your eyes.

174. May God satisfy your mouth with good things.

175. May the Lord give you food in due season.

176. May God bring you out with joy and gladness.

177. May God show you His honorable and glorious works.

178. May you remember His wonderful works.

179. May the Lord be gracious and full of compassion towards you.

180. May the Lord send redemption to you.

181. May you know that the fear of the Lord is the beginning of wisdom.

182. May God give you a good understanding.

183. May God seat you with princes.

184. May the Lord deliver your soul.

185. May the Lord deliver you from death, your eyes from tears and your feet from falling.

186. May you walk before the Lord in the land of the living.

187. May God show you His merciful kindness and His truth that endures forever.

188. May you know that the Lord is on your side and not fear what man can do to you.

189. May you know that God is for you.

190. May you put your trust in the Lord and not in man or princes.

191. May the Lord be your strength and song and your salvation.

192. May you declare the works of the Lord.

193. May you keep His testimonies and seek Him with your whole heart.

194. May you walk in His ways and keep His precepts.

195. May God remove reproach and contempt from you.

196. May you meditate on His statutes.

197. May God turn your eyes from looking at worthless things and revive you in His way.

198. May God establish His word to you.

199. May your heart be blameless and not be ashamed.

200. May God revive you according to His loving kindness.

201. May God deliver you from the oppression of man.

202. May the Lord give you understanding that you may live.

203. May God keep you from stumbling.

204. May the Lord be your keeper and your shade at your right hand.

205. May the Lord preserve you from all evil.

206. May God preserve your soul.

207. May the Lord preserve your going out and your coming in from this time forth and even evermore.

208. May your help be in the name of the Lord.

209. May it be well with you.

210. May the Lord fill your mouth with laughter and your tongue with singing.

211. May you wait for the Lord and hope in His word.

212. May you receive the Lord's mercy and redemption.

213. May the Lord command the blessing of life evermore.

214. May the Lord judge you and have compassion on you.

215. May God remember you in your lowly state and rescue you from your enemies.

216. May the Lord answer you when you cry out.

217. May the Lord make you bold and strengthen your soul.

218. May the Lord perfect that which concerns you.

219. May the Lord hedge you behind and before, and lay His hand upon you.

220. May you know that you are fearfully and wonderfully made.

221. May you know the thoughts of the Lord.

222. May God search you and know your heart, try you and know your anxieties.

223. May God see if there is any wicked way in you and lead you in the everlasting way.

224. May God deliver you from evil men and preserve you from violent men.

225. May the Lord keep you from the hands of the wicked who have purposed to make your steps stumble.

226. May God cover your head in the day of battle.

227. May the Lord give ear to your voice when you cry out to Him.

228. May your prayer be set before the Lord as incense and the lifting up of your hands as the evening sacrifice.

229. May the Lord answer you in His faithfulness and His righteousness.

230. May you meditate on all the works of the Lord.

231. May your soul long for the Lord as in a dry and thirsty land.

232. May the Lord in His mercy cut off your enemies and destroy all who afflict your soul.

233. May you declare God's awesome acts and His greatness.

234. May you meditate on the glorious splendor of His majesty and His wondrous works.

235. May you sing of God's greatness.

236. May the Lord uphold you when you fall, and raise you up when you are bowed down.

237. May the Lord be near to you when you call upon Him.

238. May He fulfill your desires.

239. May the Lord strengthen the bars of your gates.

240. May God make peace in your borders.

241. May God establish you forever and ever.

242. May you rejoice in your Maker and be joyful in your King.

243. May you be joyful in the Lord.

244. May the high praises of God be in your mouth.

245. May you praise Him with the timbrel and dance, and praise Him with stringed instruments and flutes.

246. May you perceive words of understanding and receive the instruction of wisdom, justice and judgment.

247. May you be prudent and discreet.

248. May you be like the wise man who hears and increases learning.

249. May you hearken unto the voice of wisdom, dwell safely and be quiet from fear of evil.

250. May you lie down and not be afraid.

251. May you receive the teaching of the Lord, and may the years of your life be many.

252. May all your ways be established. May you not turn to the right hand or the left.

253. May your eyes look straight ahead, and may you ponder the path of your feet.

254. May you pay attention to the wisdom of the Lord and listen to His understanding.

255. May you regard discretion, and may your lips keep knowledge.

256. May you keep the words of the Lord, treasure His commandments, and live.

257. May you have the Lord's counsel and sound wisdom.

258. May the Lord lead you in the way of righteousness and in the paths of judgment.

259. May you hear instruction, be wise and heed it.

260. May the Lord give you the dew of heaven.

261. May your mouth be a well of life.
May you store up knowledge.

262. May you listen to counsel
and be wise.

263. May you have a wise tongue
that promotes health.

264. May you be a counselor of peace,
and may your words
be established forever.

265. May diligence be your
precious possession.

266. May righteousness
guard you.

267. May you be satisfied
from above.

268. May you be prudent and
consider your steps well.

269. May your table be set with love
and peace and joy.

270. May the Lord direct
your steps.

271. May you have a
heart of wisdom.

272. May you speak pleasant words
that are like honeycomb and
health to the bones.

273. May you not be deceived
by strong drink.

274. May you hear counsel and receive instruction that you may be wise in your later years.

275. May you have discretion, be slow to anger and overlook transgression.

276. May you cease from strife.

277. May you walk wisely and be delivered.

278. May you open your mouth and judge righteously, and may you plead the cause of the poor and needy.

279. May you extend your hand to the poor, and reach out to the needy.

280. May strength and honor be your clothing and may you rejoice in the future.

281. May you open your mouth with wisdom, and may the law of kindness be on your tongue.

282. May you excel in all you do and receive the fruit of your hands.

283. May your own works praise you.

284. May you understand the times and the seasons.

285. May you walk prudently when you go before the Lord.

286. May you draw near to hear, rather than to give the sacrifice of fools.

287. May you be transformed by the renewing of your mind, and may you prove the good and acceptable and perfect will of God.

288. May all you do be done with love.

289. May the God and Father of our Lord Jesus Christ, the Father of mercies and God of all comfort, comfort you in all your trouble.

290. May you be able to comfort those who are in any trouble with the comfort with which you have been comforted by God.

291. May you walk wisely, redeeming the time.

292. May you understand what the will of the Lord is.

293. May you be strong in the Lord and in the power of His might.

294. May you be able to stand against the wiles of the devil.

295. May you be filled with the fruits of righteousness.

296. May you be encouraged.

297. May you be anxious for nothing, but in everything by prayer and supplication, with thanksgiving, let your requests be made known to God.

298. May the peace of God, which surpasses all understanding, guard your heart and mind through Christ Jesus.

299. May you learn to be content.

300. May you seek those things which are above, where Christ is sitting at the right hand of God.

301. May the word of Christ dwell in you richly in all wisdom.

302. May you be known for your work of faith, labor of love, and patience of hope in our Lord Jesus.

303. May you lead a quiet life, minding your own business.

304. May you be found blameless.

305. May you obtain a good standing and great boldness in the faith which is in Christ Jesus.

306. May you know how you ought to conduct yourself.

307. May you be nourished in the words of faith.

308. May you hold fast to the pattern of sound words in the faith and love which are in Christ Jesus.

309. May the Lord give you understanding in all things.

310. May you pursue righteousness, faith, love and peace with those who call on the Lord out of a pure heart.

311. May you speak the things which are proper.

312. May you be careful to maintain good works: the things that are good and profitable to men.

313. May you enter His rest.

314. May you obtain a good testimony through faith.

315. May you be patient, and established in your heart.

316. May you know that you were called to inherit a blessing.

317. May you proclaim the praises of Him who called you out of darkness into His marvelous light.

318. May you be adorned with the hidden person of the heart, with the incorruptible beauty of a gentle and quiet spirit which is very precious in the sight of God.

319. May you be armed with the same mind as Jesus.

320. Grace and peace be multiplied to you in the knowledge of God and of Jesus our Lord.

321. May you be found by Him to be diligent in peace, blameless, and without spot.

322. May you grow in the grace and knowledge of our Lord and Savior, Jesus Christ.

323. May you have hope, and may your heart be pure.

324. May you love in deed and in truth.

325. May you know that you have eternal life, and may you continue to believe in the name of the Son of God.

326. May you know Him who is true.

327. May you prosper in all things and be in health.

328. May you see the goodness of the Lord in the land of the living.

329. May you taste and see that the Lord is good. May you eat and be satisfied.

330. May you know and understand the excellence of His name.

331. May He keep you from the wicked who oppress and from those who speak proudly.

332. May the Lord light your lamp, and may you be a beacon to others.

333. May you see the mercy of the Lord, and may you show His great mercy to others.

334. May you know and understand His covenant.

335. May the Lord lead you and guide you for His name's sake.

336. May the Lord strengthen you
so that you may trust in Him.

337. May you be glad and
rejoice in His mercy.

338. May the Lord consider you in
your troubles, deliver you from
the hand of the enemy, and set
your feet in a wide place.

339. May the Lord guide
you with His eye.

340. May the Lord surround
you with mercy.

341. May the Lord adorn you with
beauty and cause you to rejoice.

342. May the Lord command His
loving kindness in the daytime,
and in the night may His song
be with you.

343. May the Lord vindicate you, plead
your cause, and deliver you
from the deceitful and unjust.

344. May the Lord uphold you with
His right hand, lead you with
the light of His countenance,
and give you favor.

345. May the Lord save you by His
name and vindicate you
by His strength.

346. May the Lord hear your prayer and give ear to the words of your mouth.

347. May the Lord uphold your life.

348. May the Lord repay your enemies for their evil and cut them off in His truth.

349. May you praise Him among the peoples.

350. May you sing to Him among the nations.

351. May God defend you from those who rise up against you.

352. May God deliver you from the workers of iniquity and save you from bloodthirsty men.

353. May you trust in the Lord at all times.

354. May you seek the Lord early.

355. May you thirst for the Lord.

356. May you praise the Lord with joyful lips.

357. May you remember the Lord on your bed and meditate on Him in the night watches.

358. May you rejoice in the shadow of His wings.

359. May the Lord hide you from the secret plots of the wicked.

360. May you be glad in the Lord and trust in Him.

361. May God answer you by awesome deeds in righteousness.

362. May you bless God in the congregations.

363. May the Lord deliver you from those who hate you.

364. May the Lord show His face to you and hear you speedily.

365. May the Lord draw you near and redeem you.

366. May the Lord deliver you from your enemies.

367. May the Lord be your help and deliverer.

368. May the Lord deliver you and cause you to escape.

369. May you know Him who says, "I will never leave you nor forsake you."

370. May you declare His strength to this generation and His power to everyone who is to come.

371. May God comfort your soul.

372. In the night, may God bring to remembrance your song.

373. May God reveal Himself to the generation to come that they might know Him.

374. May you remember the wonders of God.

375. May you remember that God is your rock and redeemer.

376. May God free you from the hand of the wicked.

377. May God show you His mercy and grant His salvation.

378. May God allow you to hear what He speaks.

379. May God keep you from turning back to folly.

380. May God bow down His ear to you.

381. May all your prayers come before God.

382. May you be exalted in God's righteousness.

383. May you receive God's loving kindness and faithfulness.

384. May God instruct you and teach you.

385. May you be thankful to Him and bless His name.

386. May you give thanks to the Lord and call upon His name.

387. May you make known His deeds among the peoples.

388. May you remember His marvelous works which He has done.

389. May the Lord send the rod of His strength to you to rule in the midst of His enemies.

390. May the Lord be your portion.

391. May you love the pure word of the Lord.

392. May the Lord seek you like a lost sheep.

393. May the Lord revive you according to His justice.

394. May the Lord consider your affliction and deliver you.

395. May the Lord plead your cause and redeem you and revive you according to His word.

396. May God grant you His tender mercies.

397. May the Lord deliver your soul from lying lips and a deceitful tongue.

398. May you experience the safety of a multitude of counselors.

399. May you follow instructions from the Lord, and may your righteous statements bless others.

400. May your words be established forever.

401. May you bring counsel of peace and joy.

402. May you have a good word that makes glad and lifts the heart of the anxious.

403. May you seek out wise friends and be wise yourself.

404. May you have the tongue of the wise and have soft answers to turn away wrath.

405. May you seek counsel, and may your purposes be established.

406. May your ear hear the reproofs of life; may you live among the wise and get understanding.

407. May you receive the reproof given to you.

408. May you have friends and be friendly; may you know the friend that sticks closer than a brother.

409. May you give bread and water to your enemies and may the Lord reward you.

410. May you be sharpened by the countenance of your friends.

411. May you comfort those who are oppressed.

412. May you conduct yourself in the world in simplicity and godly sincerity.

413. May you understand the access you have to the Father.

414. May you open your mouth boldly to make known the mysteries of the gospel.

415. May you be bold to speak the word without fear.

416. May you lay hold of that for which Christ Jesus has laid hold of you.

417. May you walk as a child of the light and as a child of the day.

418. May your faith grow exceedingly.

419. May you walk in wisdom toward those who are outside, redeeming the time.

420. May your speech always be with grace and seasoned with salt that you may know how you ought to answer.

421. May you walk properly toward those who are outside, and may you lack nothing.

422. May you comfort the fainthearted, uphold the weak, and be patient with all.

423. May the love of every one of you all abound toward each other.

424. May you have a good testimony among those who are outside.

425. May you be gentle to all, able to teach and be patient.

426. May you learn to maintain good works, to meet urgent needs and be fruitful.

427. May you draw near to Him with a true heart in full assurance of faith.

428. May you hold fast the confession of your hope without wavering, for He who promised is faithful.

429. May you consider one another in order to stir up love and good works.

430. May the genuineness of your faith, which is much more precious than gold that perishes, be found worthy of praise, honor and glory at the revelation of Jesus Christ.

431. May you have compassion for one another: love as brothers, be tenderhearted and courteous.

432. May you have fervent love for one another.

433. May you be made glad and triumph through the work God has given you.

434. May you be diligent in your business and may you stand before kings.

435. May God keep you busy with the joy of your heart.

436. May you enjoy the portion and the labor allotted to you.

437. May wisdom bring you success.

438. May you not lack in any gift.

439. May your
work endure.

440. May you receive
your full reward.

441. May you devote yourself to
the ministry of the saints.

442. May you not lose heart.
May you reap in due season.

443. May the Lord delight in you and
bring you into a broad place.

444. May the Lord make your way
perfect and uphold you with
His right hand.

445. May His gentleness
make you great.

446. May He grant you according to
your heart's desire and fulfill all
of your purpose.

447. May the Lord fulfill
all your petitions.

448. May goodness and mercy follow
you all the days of your life.

449. May you walk in paths
of mercy and truth.

450. May your foot stand
in an even place.

451. May you be free from fear and
always confident in the Lord.

452. May you know the mercy
of the Lord in the heavens.

453. May you know His faithfulness
that reaches to the clouds.

454. May you be abundantly satisfied
with the fullness of His house.

455. May you drink from the river
of His pleasures.

456. May you delight yourself in the
Lord, and may He give you
the desires of your heart.

457. May you commit your way to the
Lord and trust in Him that He
may bring it to pass.

458. May He bring forth your
righteousness as the light, and
your justice as the noonday.

459. May you rest in the Lord and wait
patiently for Him.

460. May the Lord order your steps
and delight in your way.

461. May the Lord uphold
you with His hand.

462. May your future be
filled with peace.

463. May the Lord make
haste to help you.

464. May you wait on the Lord and keep His way, and may He exalt you to inherit the land.

465. May the Lord arise and redeem you for His mercy's sake.

466. May the Lord anoint you with the oil of gladness.

467. May the Lord be your refuge and strength, a present help in time of trouble.

468. May the Lord have mercy upon you according to His loving kindness and according to the multitude of His tender mercies.

469. May you call upon God and may the Lord save you.

470. May you cast your burden on the Lord.

471. May you render praises to Him.

472. May you make your refuge in the shadow of His wings.

473. May you see the works of God.

474. May God exalt you and be your judge.

475. May the Lord be the object of your desire.

476. May He be your strength and portion forever.

477. May God show you His wonders.

478. May your soul long for the courts of the Lord.

479. May God grant you grace and glory and all good things.

480. May God revive you.

481. May God establish the work of your hands.

482. May you dwell in the secret place of the Most High and abide under the shadow of the Almighty.

483. May you flourish like a palm tree and grow like a cedar in Lebanon.

484. May judgment return to righteousness.

485. May you exalt the Lord and worship at His footstool.

486. May your meditation be sweet to the Lord.

487. May God satisfy your longing soul and fill you with goodness.

488. May He calm the storm so that its waves are still, and may He guide you to your desired haven.

489. May your heart be steadfast and may you sing and give praise.

490. May you take up the cup of salvation and call upon the name of the Lord.

491. May you pay your vows to the Lord in the presence of all His people.

492. May you call upon the Lord in your distress and may He answer you and set you in a broad place.

493. May God deal bountifully with you so you may live and keep His word.

494. May God revive you according to His word.

495. May God teach you His statutes.

496. May God give you understanding to keep His law.

497. May God make you walk in the path of His commandments.

498. May God cause you to walk in liberty.

499. May the word of the Lord give you life.

500. May you keep God's righteous judgments.

501. May you be single-minded.

502. May God be your hiding place and shield.

503. May God deal with you according to His mercy and teach you His statutes.

504. May God look upon you and be merciful.

505. May you eat the labor of your hands and be happy.

506. May you walk in all your ways safely and may your foot never stumble.

507. May the Lord be your confidence and keep you from fear.

508. May you know the excellence of wisdom.

509. May only wise words come from your lips.

510. May you call wisdom your sister and understanding your nearest kin.

511. May the reproofs of instruction be your way of life, and may they keep you from evil. When you roam, may they lead you; when you sleep, may they keep you; when you awake, may they speak with you.

512. May you hear wisdom crying out to you and understanding speaking to you.

513. May you have wisdom that is better than rubies, and may you find knowledge.

514. May you forsake foolishness, and live and walk in the way of understanding.

515. May you receive the sure reward of one who sows righteousness.

516. May you be wise and reap the fruit of righteousness.

517. May you never be put to shame. May your hope never perish.

518. May you be gracious, and retain honor.

519. May you be blameless in all your ways.

520. May you trust in the Lord and flourish.

521. May you love instruction and knowledge, and obtain the favor of the Lord.

522. May you love correction.

523. May you hate lying and keep to the truth.

524. May you guard your mouth and preserve your life.

525. May you sow in the land God has given you and receive a hundredfold blessing from the Lord.

526. May you have the wisdom of the prudent.

527. May you fear the Lord and depart from evil.

528. May you be prudent and crowned with knowledge.

529. May you have a heart of understanding that seeks knowledge.

530. May the Lord delight in your prayers.

531. May the Lord establish your boundaries.

532. May you have the heart of the righteous and give thought to your answers.

533. May you have joy by the answer of your mouth, and may it be filled with good words spoken in due season.

534. May your heart be pure and your words pleasant.

535. May you run and not be weary. May you walk and not faint.

536. May you walk in the ways of the Lord, and not in your own ways.

537. May you rule your spirit and be slow to anger.

538. May your ways please the Lord, and may even your enemies be at peace with you.

539. May you wisely heed the word.

540. May you trust in the Lord and be contented.

541. May you love at all times and be a friend.

542. May the name of the Lord be your strong tower.

543. May the wisdom of the Lord be like a well in your heart, and may many come and draw from it.

544. May you be a faithful witness.

545. May you get wisdom and keep understanding.

546. May you have pity upon the poor.

547. May you remember to be kind.

548. May your purposes be established by counsel and with good advice.

549. May mercy and truth preserve you.

550. May the Lord reveal His will to you.

551. May you hear the cries of the poor.

552. May you follow righteousness and mercy and find life, righteousness and honor.

553. May you be generous and be blessed.

554. May you cease from your own wisdom.

555. May you guard your mouth and tongue, and keep your soul from troubles.

556. May you be humble, fear the Lord, and receive riches and honor and life.

557. May you apply your heart to instruction and your ears to the words of knowledge.

558. May you not envy sinners, but fear the Lord all of your days.

559. May you buy the truth and not sell it—also wisdom, instruction, and understanding.

560. May your house be built through wisdom. May it be established by understanding, and may its rooms be filled with all good things.

561. May you receive your reward and may your hope be fulfilled.

562. May you be strong and not faint in the day of adversity.

563. May you search out matters that God has concealed.

564. May the Lord promote you and not you yourself.

565. May your words be well spoken,
like apples of gold in pictures
of silver.

566. May you be a faithful messenger
and refresh the soul of
your master.

567. May you rule over
your own spirit.

568. May you be as bold
as a lion.

569. May you be one who seeks the
Lord and understands all things.

570. May you be faithful and abound
with blessings.

571. May you have vision
and revelation.

572. May the Lord give you the grace
to eat the blessings given to you.

573. May God grant you the ability to
enjoy the fruit of your labors.

574. May you receive your heritage
and rejoice in it.

575. May you eat your bread with joy,
and drink your wine with
a merry heart.

576. May your garments always be
white, and may your head
lack no oil.

577. May your words be gracious.

578. May your faith be spoken of throughout the world.

579. May you not waver at the promise of God, but be strengthened in faith and fully convinced that what He has promised He is able to perform.

580. May you be conformed to the image of God's Son.

581. May you believe on Him and not be put to shame.

582. May you know the depth of the riches of both the wisdom and the knowledge of God.

583. May the God of patience and comfort grant you to be like-minded toward one another, according to Christ Jesus, that you may with one mind and one mouth glorify the God and Father of our Lord Jesus Christ.

584. May the Lord enrich you in everything.

585. May your faith rest not in the wisdom of men, but in the power of God.

586. Now may the God of hope fill you with all joy and peace in believing, that you may abound in hope by the power of the Holy Spirit.

587. May the Lord confirm you to the end, and present you blameless in the day of our Lord Jesus Christ.

588. May you speak the word in power and demonstration of the Spirit.

589. May you know the things that have been freely given to you by God.

590. May you grow up into Him in all wisdom and prudence.

591. May you be considered a servant of Christ and a steward of the mysteries of God.

592. May you be found faithful.

593. May you run the race well and receive the prize.

594. May you be an imitator of God.

595. May you pursue love and desire spiritual gifts.

596. May you bear the image of the heavenly Man.

597. May you know that your labor is not in vain in the Lord.

598. May you stand fast in the faith, and be brave and strong.

599. May the grace of God be abundant toward you.

600. May you say yes to all the promises of God.

601. May you not lose heart, and may your inward man be renewed day by day.

602. May you abound in everything— in faith, in speech, in knowledge, in all diligence, and love.

603. May the Lord commend you.

604. May the power of Christ rest upon you.

605. May you be of good comfort, of one mind, live in peace, and may the God of love and peace be with you.

606. May you know the simplicity that is in Christ.

607. May you stand fast in the liberty by which you have been set free.

608. May you walk in the Spirit and be led by Him.

609. May the fruit of the Spirit be abundant in your life.

610. May you not grow weary in well doing.

611. May peace and mercy be upon you.

612. May you stand before Him, holy and blameless.

613. May you receive fully your inheritance in Him.

614. May you be rooted and grounded in love.

615. May you have the joy that is unspeakable and full of glory.

616. May you possess the peace that passes understanding.

617. May you know the love of Christ which passes knowledge.

618. May you be filled with all the fullness of God.

619. May you walk worthy of your calling.

620. May you fully realize the grace that is given to you according to the gift of Christ.

621. May you speak the truth in love, and grow up in all things into Him who is the head.

622. May you be renewed in the spirit of your mind.

623. May no corrupt word proceed out of your mouth.

624. May you impart grace to those who hear you.

625. May you be kind, tenderhearted and forgiving.

626. May you walk in love, as Christ has loved you.

627. May you walk as a child of light.

628. May you be filled with the Spirit.

629. May you be confident that He who has begun a good work in you will complete it.

630. May your love abound more and more in knowledge and discernment.

631. May you be sincere and without offense until the day of Christ.

632. May you do all things without complaining or disputing.

633. May you shine as a light in the world.

634. May you hold fast to the word of life.

635. May your proven character be known.

636. May you forget those things which lie behind.

637. May you press toward the goal for the prize of the upward call of God in Christ Jesus.

638. May your gentleness be known to all men.

639. May you continue in the faith, grounded and steadfast.

640. May your hearts be encouraged and knit together in love.

641. May you be rooted and built up in Him and established in the faith.

642. May you set your mind on things above, not on things on the earth.

643. May the peace of God rule in your heart, and may you be thankful.

644. May you take heed to the ministry which you have received in the Lord, and you may fulfill it.

645. May you be an example to all who believe.

646. May the word of the Lord sound forth from you in every place.

647. May you speak, not as pleasing men, but pleasing God who tests the heart.

648. May you abound more and more, walking in the way, pleasing God.

649. May you possess your own vessel in sanctification and honor.

650. May you be as those who are of the day, sober, wearing the breastplate of faith and love, and as a helmet the hope of salvation.

651. May you rejoice always, pray without ceasing, and in everything give thanks.

652. May you test all things and hold fast to what is good.

653. May you not be soon shaken in mind or troubled in spirit.

654. May you obey the Lord in love from a pure heart, a good conscience and sincere faith.

655. May the Lord enable you to do His will, and may He count you faithful.

656. May you continue in faith, love, and holiness, with self-control.

657. May your progress be evident to all.

658. May you be counted worthy of double honor.

659. May you serve the Lord without prejudice or partiality.

660. May your good works be clearly evident.

661. May you pursue righteousness, godliness, faith, love, patience and gentleness.

662. May you guard what is committed to your trust.

663. May you stir up the gift of God which is in you.

664. May you walk in the spirit of power, love and a sound mind.

665. May you be strong in the grace that is in Christ Jesus.

666. May you endure hardship as a good soldier of Jesus Christ.

667. May you be a vessel for honor, sanctified and useful for the Master, prepared for every good work.

668. May you be ready in season and out.

669. May you be watchful in all things, endure afflictions, and fulfill your ministry.

670. May you be hospitable, a lover of what is good, sober-minded, just, holy and self-controlled, holding fast the faithful word.

671. May the Lord pour out upon you abundantly His mercy, kindness and love.

672. May you have great joy and consolation in your love, and may you be refreshed.

673. May you hold the beginning of your confidence steadfast to the end.

674. May you patiently endure and obtain what He has promised you.

675. May hope anchor your soul.

676. May you be of full age, highly skilled in the word of righteousness, and trained to discern both good and evil.

677. May you show the same diligence to the full assurance of hope until the end, and imitate those who through faith and patience inherit the promises.

678. May the Lord put His law into your heart and write it in your mind.

679. May your confidence be greatly rewarded.

680. May you always please the Lord and be rewarded as one who diligently seeks Him.

681. May you know the steadfast love of the Lord.

682. May you have grace, and serve God acceptably with reverence and godly fear.

683. May you be perfect and complete, lacking nothing.

684. May your faith be revealed by your works.

685. May you show by good conduct that your works are done in the meekness of wisdom.

686. Now may the God of peace who brought up our Lord Jesus from the dead, that great Shepherd of the sheep, through the blood of the everlasting covenant, make you complete in every good work to do His will, working in you what is well pleasing in His sight.

687. May you have the wisdom that is from above, pure, peaceable, gentle, willing to yield, full of mercy and good fruits, without partiality and without hypocrisy.

688. May the Lord give you grace.

689. May the Lord lift you up.

690. May you be holy in all your conduct.

691. May you be a good steward of the manifold grace of God.

692. May you neither be barren nor unfruitful in the knowledge of our Lord Jesus Christ.

693. May you never stumble.

694. May you walk in the light
as He is in the light.

695. May you abide in Him
and walk as He walked.

696. May the word of God abide in
you and give you strength.

697. May you have the victory that
overcomes the world.

698. May you receive
a full reward.

699. May you be like Abraham,
the friend of God.

700. May you be like Moses, who
spoke to God face to face.

701. May you be like David, one who
is after the heart of God.

702. May you walk
in the truth.

703. Mercy, peace, and love
be multiplied to you.

704. May you know your inheritance in
Him, and His inheritance
in you.

705. May you serve the purposes
of God in your generation.

706. May you see the blessing of those
who put their trust in the Lord.

707. May the Lord lead you in His righteousness and make His way straight before you.

708. May the Lord consider you and hear you and enlighten your eyes.

709. May you trust in His mercy and rejoice in His salvation.

710. May you sing to the Lord because He has dealt bountifully with you.

711. May you abide in the Lord and fear Him.

712. May you walk uprightly, work righteousness, and speak truth in your heart.

713. May the Lord give you counsel and instruct you in the night seasons.

714. May you always set the Lord before you.

715. May your heart be glad, and may you rest in hope.

716. May He incline His ear to you and hear your words.

717. May you see His face in righteousness and be satisfied when you awake in His likeness.

718. May He show you the path of life, for in His presence is fullness of joy and at His right hand there are pleasures forevermore.

719. May he show you His marvelous loving kindness, keep you as the apple of His eye, and hide you under the shadow of His wings.

720. May the Lord be your strength, your rock and your fortress.

721. May that which is more desirable than gold and sweeter than honey be yours.

722. May the words of your mouth and the meditations of your heart be acceptable in His sight.

723. May you rise and stand upright.

724. May you have joy in His strength, and may you greatly rejoice in His salvation.

725. May He give you your heart's desire and not withhold the request of your lips.

726. May you receive the honor that comes only from God.

727. May the Lord bless you forever and make you exceedingly glad with His presence.

728. May the Lord meet you with blessings of goodness, and set a crown of pure gold upon your head.

729. May you put your trust in the Lord and His mercy, and may you not be moved.

730. May the Lord be with you.

731. May you fear no evil.

732. May His rod and His staff comfort you.

733. May the Lord show you His ways and teach you His paths.

734. May the Lord lead you and teach you in His truth, and may you wait only for Him.

735. May the Lord remember His tender mercy and His loving kindness toward you.

736. May He guide you in justice and teach you His way.

737. May you fear the Lord.

738. May He teach you to walk in the way He chooses.

739. May you fear the Lord and know His secrets.

740. May He show you His covenant.

741. May your eyes ever be toward the Lord, and may He pluck your feet out of the net.

742. May you proclaim the Lord with the voice of thanksgiving, and tell of all His wondrous works.

743. May the Lord redeem you and be merciful to you.

744. May you see the beauty of the Lord.

745. May the Lord teach you His way and lead you in a smooth path.

746. May you remember the name of the Lord.

747. May the Lord turn your mourning into dancing.

748. May the Lord give you His favor for life and fill you with joy.

749. May the Lord be your rock of refuge and fortress of defense.

750. May you never be put to shame and may the Lord deliver you in His righteousness.

751. May the Lord make His face to shine upon you and save you for His mercy's sake.

752. May you know the goodness that the Lord has laid up for those that fear Him.

753. May the Lord hide you in the secret place of His presence.

754. May the Lord hear the voice of your supplication when you cry to Him.

755. May you know that when He speaks it is done and when He commands it shall stand fast.

756. May the Lord be your counselor and show you the plans of His heart.

757. May His mercy be upon you as you trust in Him.

758. May the Lord vindicate you in His righteousness.

759. May your tongue speak of His righteousness.

760. May you praise Him all the day long.

761. May you cease from anger, forsake wrath, and fret not.

762. May you know the Lord, and may He continue His loving kindness toward you.

763. May you delight yourself in the abundance of peace.

764. May the law of God be in your heart.

765. May the Lord deliver you from all your transgressions, and may you be free of all reproach.

766. May His loving kindness and truth continually preserve you.

767. May the Lord make haste to help you.

768. May the Lord deliver you in time of trouble.

769. May the Lord command victories for you.

770. May your heart not turn back, nor your steps depart from His way.

771. May the Lord make you hear joy and gladness.

772. May your heart be clean and your spirit steadfast.

773. May you have the joy of your salvation restored to you and be upheld by His generous spirit.

774. May you be like a green olive tree in the house of God and may you trust in the mercy of God forever and ever.

775. May God attend to you and hear you.

776. May God send from heaven and save you.

777. May God send forth His mercy and His truth.

778. May God be your strength and defense.

779. May the God of mercy come to meet you.

780. May the Lord be your refuge in the day of your trouble.

781. May the Lord hear your voice and preserve your life from fear of the enemy.

782. May you know the ways of God.

783. May God give you strength and power.

784. May God arise and have mercy on you.

785. May the Lord hear you in the acceptable time in the multitude of His mercy.

786. May the Lord guide you with His counsel and receive you into glory.

787. May you walk in the light of God's countenance.

788. May He deliver you out of the hand of the wicked.

789. May you serve the Lord with gladness and come before His presence with singing.

790. May you know that you are one of His people and of the sheep of His pasture.

791. May God hear you when you call and answer you speedily.

792. May God redeem your life from destruction.

793. May God crown you with loving kindness and tender mercies.

794. May the Lord execute righteousness and justice for you.

795. May God make His ways and acts known to you.

796. May God remember you with His favor and visit you with His salvation.

797. May God regard your affliction and hear your cry.

798. May God redeem you from the hand of the enemy.

799. May God lead you forth by the right way.

800. May God bring you out of darkness and the shadow of death and break your chains in pieces.

801. May God send His word and heal you and deliver you from destruction.

802. May God cause you to do valiantly.

803. May the Lord deal with you for His name's sake.

804. May you fear the Lord and be blessed and greatly delight in His commandments.

805. May God loose your bonds.

806. May God direct your ways.

807. May God not allow you to wander from His commandments.

808. May you meditate on His precepts and ways.

809. May you delight yourself in His statutes and not forget His word.

810. May God open your eyes that you may see wondrous things from His law.

811. May God turn away your reproach.

812. May God revive you in His righteousness.

813. May you remember the name of the Lord in the night.

814. May God be merciful to you according to His word.

815. May God give you understanding that you may learn His commandments.

816. May God's word be a lamp to your feet and a light to your path.

817. May God give you understanding.

818. May you hate every false way.

819. May God's face shine upon you.

820. May the hand of the Lord become your help.

821. May the Lord surround you from this time forth and forever.

822. May the Lord do great things for you.

823. May you fear the Lord and walk in His ways.

824. May you receive the forgiveness of the Lord.

825. May you be calm and may your soul be quieted.

826. May the Lord regard your lowly state.

827. May the Lord revive you when you walk in the midst of trouble.

828. May His right hand save you.

829. May the right hand of the Lord lead you and hold you.

830. May you know that you were formed by His hands in your mother's womb.

831. May you put your eyes on the Lord and take refuge in Him.

832. May the Lord set a guard over your mouth and keep watch over the door of your lips.

833. May the Lord keep you from the snares laid for you and from the traps of the workers of iniquity.

834. May the Lord attend to your cry and deliver you from your persecutors.

835. May the Lord hear your prayer and give ear to your supplications.

836. May the Lord cause you to hear His loving kindness in the morning.

837. May the Lord cause you to know the way in which to walk.

838. May you take shelter in the Lord.

839. May God teach you to do His will.

840. May the Lord revive you for His name's sake.

841. May the Lord be your high tower and deliverer, your shield and the One in whom you take refuge.

842. May you know that the Lord is gracious and full of compassion, slow to anger and great in mercy.

843. May you know that the Lord is good to all, and His tender mercies are over all His works.

844. May the Lord take pleasure in you.

845. May you choose the fear of the Lord and embrace His counsel.

846. May you receive His words and hide His commandments within you.

847. May your ear be inclined to wisdom, and your heart applied to understanding.

848. May you understand the fear of the Lord and find the knowledge of God.

849. May you understand righteousness, judgment, equity and every good path.

850. May wisdom enter into your heart and knowledge be pleasant to your soul.

851. May you walk in the way of good men and keep the paths of the righteous.

852. May discretion preserve you and understanding keep you, and may they deliver you from the way of the evil man.

853. May you remember the ways of the Lord. May they add long life and peace to you.

854. May you not forsake mercy and truth, may you bind them around your neck and write them upon the table of your heart.

855. May you find favor and good understanding in the sight of God and man.

856. May you acknowledge Him in all your ways, and may He direct your paths.

857. May you trust in the Lord with all your heart and lean not to your own understanding.

858. May you honor the Lord with the first fruits of your increase.

859. May sound wisdom and discretion not depart from you. May they be life to your soul and grace to your neck.

860. May you be led in right paths, and may your steps not be hindered.

861. May you not stumble when you run.

862. May you be a delight to the Lord.

863. May you keep your heart with all diligence, for out of it are the issues of life.

864. May you be generous and freely water others.

865. May you accept reproof and be honored.

866. May your gift make room for you.

867. May you commit your works to the Lord, and may your thoughts be established.

868. May the Lord be a shield to you as you put your trust in Him.

869. May your praise come from God.

870. May you reign with Him.

871. May you be steadfast, immovable, always abounding in the work of the Lord.

872. May the Lord open great and effective doors for you.

873. May the Lord establish and anoint you.

874. May you be the fragrance of Christ.

875. May the life of Jesus be manifested in you.

876. May you be well pleasing to Him.

877. May His strength be made perfect in your weakness.

878. May God reveal His Son in you.

879. May the Lord show you opportunities to do good.

880. May the God of our Lord Jesus Christ, the Father of glory, give to you the spirit of wisdom and revelation in the knowledge of Him.

881. May you know the riches of the glory of His inheritance in the saints.

882. May the eyes of your understanding be enlightened, and may you know what is the hope of His calling.

883. May you know the working of His mighty power.

884. May He show you His kindness and the richness of His grace.

885. May you come to full maturity in the Lord.

886. May He grant you, according to the riches of His glory, to be strengthened with might through His Spirit in your inner man.

887. May the Lord work in you both to will and to do His good pleasure.

888. May you become blameless and harmless, a child of God without fault in the midst of a crooked and perverse generation.

889. May you be filled with the knowledge of His will in all wisdom and spiritual understanding.

890. May you walk worthy of the Lord, fully pleasing Him, being fruitful in every good work and increasing in the knowledge of God.

891. May you be strengthened with all might, according to His glorious power.

892. May the Lord make known to you the riches of the glory of His mystery.

893. May Christ establish you and encourage your faith.

894. May you walk worthy of God who calls you into His own kingdom and glory.

895. May the Lord make you increase and abound in love to one another and to all.

896. May He establish your heart blameless in holiness before our God and Father at the coming of our Lord Jesus Christ with all His saints.

897. May the God of peace Himself sanctify you completely.

898. May your whole spirit, soul, and body be preserved blameless at the coming of our Lord Jesus Christ.

899. Now may our Lord Jesus Christ Himself, and our God and Father, who has loved us and given us everlasting consolation and good hope by grace, comfort your hearts and establish you in every good word and work.

900. May the Lord, who is faithful, establish you and guard you from the evil one.

901. May the Lord stand with you and strengthen you.

902. Now may the Lord direct your hearts into the love of God and into the patience of Christ.

903. Now may the Lord of peace Himself give you peace always in every way.

904. May the grace of our Lord be exceedingly abundant to you, with the faith and love which are in Christ Jesus.

905. May you know whom you have believed and be persuaded that He is able to keep what you have committed to Him.

906. May you be diligent to present yourself approved to God, a worker who does not need to be ashamed, rightly dividing the word of truth.

907. May you fight the good fight, finish the race, and keep the faith.

908. May you be swift to hear, slow to speak and slow to anger.

909. May the Lord deliver you from every evil work and preserve you for His heavenly kingdom.

910. May you follow the example of Jesus.

911. In all things may you show yourself to be a pattern of good works with integrity, reverence, and incorruptibility.

912. May you come boldly, without fear, to the throne of grace, and obtain mercy and find grace to help in time of need.

913. May you receive with meekness the implanted word, which is able to save your soul.

914. May you be a doer of the word, blessed in whatever you do.

915. May you desire the pure milk of the word that you may grow, and may you taste that the Lord is gracious.

916. May you minister with the ability which God supplies, that in all things God may be glorified through Jesus Christ.

917. May the God of all grace, who called us to His eternal glory by Christ Jesus, perfect, establish, strengthen, and settle you.

918. May you know the Father and overcome the wicked one.

919. May you imitate what is good.

920. May the Lord reveal Himself to you. May you be like Him and see Him as He is.

921. May you have confidence toward God. May you know His heart.

922. May you remember the word of the Lord.

923. May the Lord increase you a thousand fold, and bless you as He has promised.

924. May you be like a tree planted by the waters.

925. May you bring forth fruit in season.

926. May you prosper in whatever you do.

927. May you know the Lord as your shepherd, and may you never lack anything.

928. May the Lord uphold you, and give you your eternal inheritance.

929. May you inherit the land and dwell in it forever.

930. May the Lord crown your year with His goodness and may your paths drip with abundance.

931. May God bless you with prosperity.

932. May the Lord give you what is good.

933. May you rejoice in His inheritance.

934. May God bless your generation with wealth and riches and His righteousness forever.

935. May the Lord deal bountifully with you.

936. May God's law be better to you than thousands of coins of gold and silver.

937. May the Lord be your portion in the land of the living.

938. May your barns be full, supplying all kinds of produce.

939. May your sheep bring forth thousands and ten thousands in your fields.

940. May your eyes look expectantly to Him. May God give you your food in due season.

941. May it be restored to you seven times what the enemy has stolen.

942. May your barns be filled with plenty and your presses burst out with new wine.

943. May you inherit the substance and treasures the Lord has for you.

944. May the Lord bless you and make you rich in every way.

945. May you eat well by the fruit of your mouth.

946. May you have mercy on the poor and be blessed.

947. May you have a merry heart and a continual feast.

948. May your thoughts lead to plenty.

949. May you have all that the Lord has allotted to you.

950. May you be rich in good works, ready to give, willing to share.

951. May you receive what He has promised you.

952. May the Lord make all grace abound to you.

953. May you always have all sufficiency in all things.

954. May you abound in every good work.

955. May He who supplies seed to the sower and bread for food, supply and multiply the seed you have sown and increase the fruits of your righteousness.

956. May this proverb be true of you, that the blessing of the Lord makes rich and He adds no sorrow to it.

957. May you see your children's children.

958. May He give you life and length of days.

959. May the Lord give you strength and bless you with peace.

960. May your days be multiplied, and years of life be added to you.

961. In health and vigor may you live out every day allotted to you.

962. May you have a merry heart—a medicine for yourself and others.

963. May you live long on the earth.

964. May God be your strong refuge.

965. May your mouth be filled with praise to the Lord.

966. May God make you glad according to the days He has given you.

967. May the Lord be gracious to you and preserve you.

968. May God direct your steps by His word and not let iniquity have dominion over you.

969. May God grant you great peace.

970. May you speak of the glory of His kingdom and talk of His power.

971. May you make known to the sons of men His mighty acts and the glorious majesty of His everlasting kingdom.

972. May the Lord preserve you.

973. May your sleep be sweet.

974. May you be slow to anger and appease strife.

975. May God deliver you out of the hand of the wicked.

976. May you triumph in the work God has given you.

977. **M**ay you be diligent in your work.

978. **M**ay you diligently seek and find wisdom.

979. **M**ay you find knowledge and wisdom. May you eat and enjoy them like honey and the honeycomb.

980. **M**ay God accept your works.

981. **M**ay you rejoice in the Lord always.

982. **M**ay you be complete, thoroughly equipped for every good work.

983. **M**ay He deliver you and be your shield, your stronghold.

984. **M**ay you walk in all the good works He has prepared for you.

985. **M**ay you stand fast in the Lord.

986. **M**ay the Lord count you worthy of His calling, and fulfill all the good pleasure of His goodness and the work of faith with power.

987. **M**ay you be fully effective in operating in the gift that is within you.

988. May you dwell in prosperity, and may your descendants inherit the earth.

989. May the Lord be merciful and gracious to you.

990. May the Lord be your shield.

991. May He clothe you with gladness.

992. May your husband love you like Christ loves the church.

993. May the Lord give you ears to hear, eyes to see, and a heart to understand what He has prepared for you.

994. May you receive all the spiritual blessings in the heavenly places.

995. May you know and understand the mysteries of the gospel.

996. May you always have all that you need.

997. May you hunger and thirst for righteousness.

998. May you be known as a peacemaker.

999. May you raise up the ancient foundations, and be known as a repairer of the breach.

1000. **M**ay your light break forth like the morning, and may the glory of the Lord be your rear guard.

1001. **M**ay you be like a well watered garden and like a spring of water that does not fail.

Index to the Blessings

This index should serve as quick reference guide and help you begin to bless. If you will occasionally browse through the list and contemplate it, you should find yourself developing a vocabulary of blessing.

Abide
695, 696, 711

Abundance
423, 570, 599, 602, 609, 648, 710, 763, 895, 930, 935, 938, 939, 942, 948, 952, 954, 956

Affliction
54, 82, 394

Anoint
466, 873

Answer
90, 216, 361, 492, 791

Beauty
165, 341, 744

Blameless
304, 321, 519, 587, 612, 631, 888, 898

Bless, Blessing, Blessed
40, 128, 143, 316, 362, 385, 553, 706, 727, 804, 923, 944, 946, 956

Faithfulness

30, 127, 138, 198, 229, 256, 312, 369, 383, 453, 491, 544, 566, 579, 655, 666, 681, 770

Family

1, 2, 3, 4, 5, 7, 8, 9, 10, 11, 45, 957

Father

13, 14, 17, 18, 22, 31, 34, 35

Favor

16, 77, 27, 32, 129, 143, 144, 189, 213, 260, 344, 364, 521, 525, 589, 716, 730, 735, 748, 751, 753, 776, 784, 787, 819, 855

Fear of the Lord

24, 120, 181, 527, 556, 558, 682, 711, 737, 739, 752, 804, 823, 845, 848

Forgiveness

64, 169, 275, 409, 625, 824

Fortress

146, 720, 749

Freedom

376, 607, 765, 800, 805

Friend

21, 408, 410, 541

Fruit, fruitful

426, 609, 692, 890, 925, 945, 1001

Goodness
111, 119, 174, 328, 329, 448, 487, 492, 533, 560, 728, 752

Grace
320, 322, 420, 479, 599, 620, 624, 665, 682, 688, 691, 884, 904, 912, 915, 917, 952, 967, 989

Gracious
179, 518, 565, 577, 842

Great
445, 882

Grow, growth
410, 418, 621, 657, 915

Guide
157, 488, 736, 745, 785, 833

Hand
820, 828, 829, 830

Healing, health
52, 64, 75, 263, 272, 327, 774, 801, 961, 962

Hear
100, 227, 228, 229, 286, 346, 378, 380, 406, 624, 708, 716, 771, 775, 781, 785, 791, 797, 835, 836, 908, 993

Heart

Help

Heritage

Holy

Home

Honor

Hope

Husband

Increase
5, 248, 858, 890, 895, 923, 955

Inheritance
23, 87, 316, 464, 613, 704, 928, 929, 933, 943, 988

Instruction
107, 246, 251, 259, 274, 384, 399, 407, 511, 521, 713, 865

Integrity
30, 157, 911

Intimacy
221, 237, 365, 699, 700, 701, 717, 762, 918

Joy
41, 80, 126, 176, 242, 243, 269, 356, 401, 435, 533, 586, 615, 672, 718, 724, 747, 748, 771, 773

Judge
214, 222, 474

Judgment
484, 500

Kindness
187, 200, 281, 342, 383, 468, 547, 625, 671, 719, 735, 762, 766, 793, 836, 884

Praise
115, 135, 170, 244, 245, 317, 349, 356, 471, 389, 760, 869, 965

Prepared
159, 668, 982

Preserve, preservation
52, 55, 60, 85, 205, 206, 207, 224, 225, 766, 781, 898, 909, 967, 972

Progress
657, 861

Promise, promises
152, 218, 579, 600, 674, 923, 951

Promote, promotion
91, 183, 236, 434, 474, 564, 689

Prosper, prosperity
5, 327, 483, 520, 576, 926, 931, 944, 988

Protection
6, 91, 118, 124, 136, 166, 167, 219, 226, 232, 266, 298, 319, 331, 340, 359, 379, 502, 542, 719, 741, 753, 821, 833, 838, 841, 900, 927

Provision
6, 338, 421, 443, 492, 493, 927, 940, 955

Prudent
247, 268, 273, 526, 528, 590

Pure, purity
47, 88, 323, 391, 534, 654

Purpose
446, 548, 705, 717

Recognition
578, 603

Redeem, redeemer, redemption
98, 151, 180, 195, 212, 291, 317, 365, 375, 395, 465, 743, 792, 798

Refreshing
45, 566, 672

Refuge
25, 82, 99, 103, 140, 146, 167, 467, 472, 780, 831, 841, 964

Regard
797, 826

Rejoice
34, 35, 73, 102, 114, 126, 163, 164, 210, 242, 244, 280, 337, 341, 358, 574, 651, 709, 724, 933, 981

Remember
83, 93, 153, 155, 178, 215, 357, 372, 374, 388, 746, 796, 809, 813, 853, 922

Renewal

65, 287, 319, 601, 622

Rest

68, 95, 303, 313, 459

Restore

58, 149, 941

Revelation

373, 550, 571, 740, 878, 880, 920

Revive

149, 197, 200, 393, 395, 480, 494, 812, 827, 840

Reward

282, 409, 440, 515, 561, 593, 637, 679, 680, 698, 728

Riches

881, 886, 892, 834

Righteousness

18, 19, 258, 266, 295, 310, 382, 458, 484, 515, 516, 532, 552, 661, 707, 717, 750, 758, 759, 794, 812, 849, 851, 934, 997

Rock

139, 146, 375, 720, 749

Safety

79, 84, 99, 106, 156, 249, 398, 482, 488, 502,

Speak
565, 588, 621, 646, 647, 755, 908

Stability
614, 653, 999

Stand
723, 901

Steadfast
489, 639, 681, 729, 755, 772, 871, 924, 985

Strength
50, 51, 56, 76, 103, 191, 293, 345, 370, 389, 467, 535, 542, 562, 579, 598, 610, 665, 696, 720, 724, 778, 783, 877, 886, 959

Strengthen
59, 92, 217, 239, 336, 476, 891, 901

Success
433, 437

Sustain
56, 66, 89, 131, 175, 204, 928

Sweet
119, 486, 721

Teach
107, 425, 495, 736, 745, 839

End Notes

Getting Started
[1] Matthew 5:44-45a

Authorized to Forgive
[1] Ephesians 4:7
[2] Genesis 2:7
[3] Romans 8:9
[4] James 1:15
[5] Luke 5:17-26
[6] Ezekiel 37:3

The Terrible Parable
[1] Matthew 18:21-35
[2] http://www.merriam-webster.com/dictionary/parable

Symptoms of Unforgiveness
[1] Romans 12:19
[2] James 3:16
[3] http://www.funtrivia.com/askft/Question74338.html

The Zero Principle
[1] Romans 8:14
[2] Matthew 18:35
[3] Romans 10:10
[4] Jeremiah 31:34
[5] Revelation 11:12

Blessing

1 The Theological Dictionary of the New Testament (Kittel's) Vol. 2, page 755
2 Genesis 27:33
3 Numbers 23:19
4 Isaiah 55:11
5 Numbers 6:22-27
6 Revelation 1:6
7 Acts 20:36
8 Acts 9:40
9 Genesis 1:28
10 Revelation 22:21
11 Luke 24:50-51
12 1 Peter 5:5
13 Acts 20:35

Questions and Objections

1 Psalm 34:1
2 Matthew 6:9-13
3 Matthew 6:14-15
4 Matthew 18:34-35
5 Genesis 50:20
6 Isaiah 61:13